NADYA RUBIN SCHUBERT

"NOTES FROM SPIRIT"

The Creating Calm Network Publishing Group

"NOTES FROM SPIRIT"

Copyright ©2014 by Nadya Rubin Schubert

Print ISBN:0615968392

Cover by Sessha Batto

First electronic publication: February 2014
First print publication: February 2014

Published in the United States of America with international distribution.

DEDICATION

Vicki White, a certified medium, spiritual counselor and my teacher, who took the time, effort and a great deal of patience to connect me with my spiritual gifts. With deepest appreciation, thank you for helping me to understand the bigger picture in all things.

Ann White, author, counselor, attorney, rabbi and radio host, who, because she saw the importance of these writings and the effect on those who read them, began to gently prod me back from my self-imposed absence in doing the work, to re-connecting with my spiritual "family", so that I may continue to bring their messages to the world by writing down the words and, in addition, giving me an opportunity to share them as a radio host on her Creating Calm Network.

The multi-generational energies that are abundantly around me for their wisdom and confidence in my ability to write down the words they want you to hear.

HOW THESE WRITINGS WERE PREPARED

Imagine a small group of people who are well-versed in spiritual philosophy, sitting around a table combining all of their thoughts. They continue to refine these thoughts until they are complete and acceptable to the entire group.

They are the ones who are writing this book. One spirit person, we shall call him the "Reader", then transmits this collaborative material to me. All of these people, other than me, live in spirit.

I receive this information in trance. As I sit by my computer, I say my affirmations to clear my mind, and enter a super-conscious state. I begin my writing by typing the first word I receive and stop when there are no more words transmitted. The entire session takes from 15-20 minutes.

I am not consciously aware of what I am writing. I do not hear the words, nor do I see them. My eyes are closed throughout. A thought comes in as a word and the flow of writing continues until there is no other thought. At that point, it feels like a veil has been lifted and I begin to slowly open my eyes and sit for a while to regain my normal breathing.

Figure 1

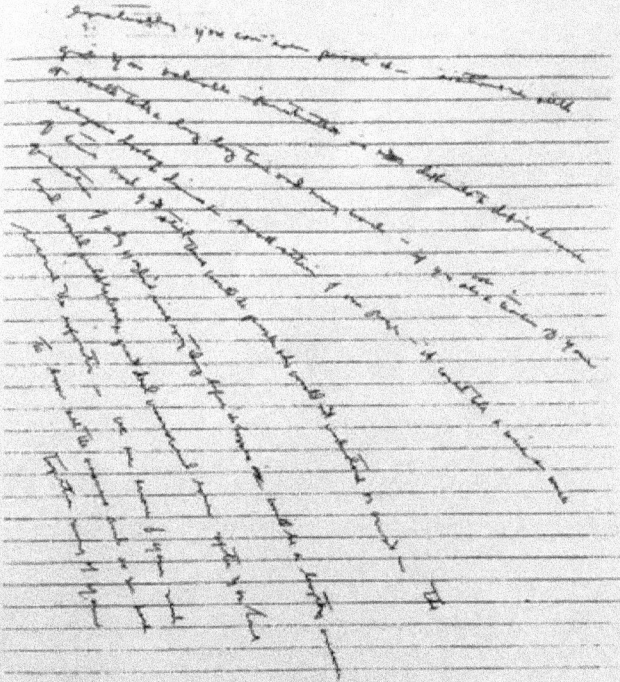

This is a sample of how I first began to write in longhand on a legal pad, going from one line to the next, in an arc, with my eyes closed.

TABLE OF CONTENTS

A Collection of Writings from the Year 2012

INTRODUCTION

It is an unusual suggestion for you to ask if you should publish our most recent writings with you at this time... we understand that you feel the interest of most people who read these writings today seem to feel more connected to them in a different way than the older writings... and because of that thought process... you would want to publish what we have brought to you in the now...

it is truly your own choice as to when you want to bring the words to the world... for you are as important as we are... and we would never hesitate to make you aware of this... you are coming into your own... more at this time... than earlier times... where you are beginning to feel comfortable with the words and how they come to you and through you to the public arena of awareness... we truly want you to be aware and feel comfortable with your input... regarding your thoughts about what you are writing... why you are writing... and not be affected by how others read or do not read... or their interpretations...

for your connection to us is to bring the writings to the world... and as quickly as you can... with that in mind... we feel these writings are extremely important and are written for the times today... exactly as they are today... we have tried to match the words with the feelings those in the material world are having as well as our own... in a manner that is more finite and direct than the earlier writings...

these writings today are meant to jiggle the mind... shake things up if you will... and wake people up to what the world has become... and will continue to become... they also need to be aware of the fact that as large groups of people gather... and discuss their issues amongst each other... they will send the messages through the ripples of their thoughts that will expand outward to all those around them and to all those around them... until there is a vast awareness that people on one side of the world are able to send to those on the other side of the world... and find that both sides of the world agree...

it will not be a surprise... as much as you think it will... for people are filled with love for their families and friends as well as their hopes and dreams for the future to be more substantial... safer... less obstructive... and more open to growth and development... a forward progression for all peoples of the land...

the true surprise may be that you find that with the many small groups melding their thinking... the coming together of those powerful groups of thoughts... will make change in the world... it has been done before and it can be done again... with patience and love and an understanding that it takes time and effort on a consistent level... never to stop... peacefully and lovingly sharing your thoughts... will bring to you the knowing that you are doing something to bring peace and balance for not only yourself... your families and your surrounding communities...

it will bring you great satisfaction to know that you are contributing your efforts to all those you do not even know and may never see... and yet you will feel the peace and love in your heart knowing that you are doing what you are only able to do... do not judge yourselves by how much time you are spending or how little it is... for it is more the quality of your efforts that will make a difference... even if it is a few minutes each day... every day that you talk it up... or write it up... in a positive and motivating way... tiny connections will be made and will build upon themselves... into the biggest bubble of energy that will travel back and forth as it gathers more and more the people that feel the comfort of that energy zone...

and as this begins to grow... you will know that you may not see changes in your physical lives at this time... yet you will understand that you are at the beginning of that wave of change that will affect everyone in the many years to come... think of yourselves as those few and strong who risked everything to come to your world hundreds of years ago... who lived very simply and with great hardship to keep their freedoms... the freedom to be who they wanted to be... writing down the words that you read today on your walls of government... and in your schools of learning... expressing their thoughts and desires to maintain the dignity of freedom within a set of guidelines...

think of all the explorers who left their zone of safety to explore and experience new lands that they felt were empty and found many people there who lived there and shared with them their languages... their food and their ideas relating to how they live... and those explorers found them so interesting in so many ways that they brought many things back to their origins to display... it was their way of connecting with other unknown people and cultures they never knew existed... and yet found comfort and beauty in what they were offered...

it does not matter if you share the world with each other through food... clothing... architecture... for that is the beginning of a peaceful connection where even though you are trading with each other your thoughts and plans... you are connecting and realizing you all have similar needs and desires and hopes for a prosperous future... and you begin to recognize that the world at large is not as large as you thought it was... as less and less becomes unfamiliar as more and more arms open to welcoming all that they have never seen or experienced before...

as we said at the beginning of this writing... we are very happy you are feeling comfortable about writing with us again... and that you would like to publish your recent writings now... and we will look forward to the outcome the writings are going to bring...

JANUARY 2

As the beginning of the new year develops... the external pressures in the world may be reduced to a simmer... and as you know... if something simmers too long it will eventually evaporate... which is our wish for all those in the material world... or... as the new year begins... things may proceed in a more daring direction... an escalation of physical disruption in those countries most vulnerable and with no dominant and healthy leadership may prevail...

it truly is never about physical duress that will solve anything... it is not a permanent solution nor a happy one... for if one needs to be physically detained or physically harmed or physically held prisoner... their thoughts will always be the way to freedom for themselves and their families... no matter what they need to do...

truly peace is the ultimate goal that will gain you the stability to maintain harmony in the world... for if the warring factions in the world today truly desire peace within their realm of existence... they would serve themselves better if they put themselves in the place of those they have kept chained to their thoughts about the leaders of their country... and would then perhaps understand the desire for freedom to be... a free thinking... creative mind without persecution is the most beautiful gift of life there is... as you see in the free countries of the world in these last few thousand years... the coming together of the wonderful tastes and smells and music of the different cultures through the many transportational inventions designed by those creative free thinkers... and on the opposite side of this... are the people of countries in the last few thousand years who have been made to sluggishly brood as they live each and every day under empirical and tyrannical leaders... with no choice other than to live as demanded... depriving them of their free will and creativity... to gather the necessary means to come together as a whole within the world... with the desire to truly know and understand that you are all from the same light...

it is all within you... and its purpose is to bring you to your higher self... so that war will be no more... and people will awake looking forward to living their day in peace... love and that driving force to create a better life... for themselves as well as those around them... we have seen how that worked for many years...

in a time long ago and a land far away... many thousands of years ago... there was a community of people who lived within that luxury of life... supporting each other with love and respect... and as the community grew... they offered the same love to others who were not of their village... things began to become a struggle... for there were differences and the newcomers did not know how to deal with them... in any other way than they were shown and that was through power... control and physical force... and so they left the community to start their own... and the seeds were laid... of frustration... and fear... and lack of developing their inner self so that all could live peacefully with their differences... learning that their differences are what made them all unique individuals... each with their own purpose that only helps to bring a stronger foundation...

we feel at this time... this mindset will be an evolutionary process waiting to happen... and that wait will unfortunately not be in this lifetime of yours... for it will take many years for all leaders to be on the same page... for all leaders to feel more confident and less superior... for all leaders to have a greater desire for peace and tranquility in their land as well as the land next to them... for as the industrial world continues... you will be only a back door away from your neighbor... living in the next country... happier or unhappier than you are... it will be that close and that available to bringing you to that place of uncertainty or calm...

we wish you all this year... the peace and love you so richly deserve... and that the eyes that are upon you are looking at you with love and the desire to share only what is for your highest good... happy new year from our light to yours.

JANUARY 9

When we write about the unhappiness and misery resulting from factions that are controlling and use their power for their own gains... whether it be monetary or satisfying their own idealism and philosophy... we do not mean to bring you to a place of uncomfortability... we want you to know that all that we bring to you is ultimately for your highest good... though you may not feel or see that at the time...

What we mean to bring to you is a thought process of knowing that in the material world... there are many possibilities... there are positive and productive ones and then there are the negative and defeating ones that only serve to bring frustration and anxiety to all those who live within that realm of thought... we also are sharing our thoughts with you in these matters of uncertain reality in your lives... so that you may allow yourself to drift from perhaps your positive rainbow like persuasion to the reality that yes you can make your world sunshine and flowers... yet in order to survive in your reality one must be aware that the other side of the coin is not as bright... and that you can learn to live within both...

It is not enough to think only that you want to remain in your positive world of thought... for truly you must embrace the fact that there are leaders who are ready to bring you down... derived from their own circumstances in life... and feeling their righteousness at all times... with no window of opportunity for others to bring change for the betterment of all mankind...

Knowing that this does exist in the world does not have to be a difficult thought for you to grasp and to allow into your thoughts... without feeling threatened that those thoughts will deter you from living your positive day... week or month... instead... you may want to begin to see that there is a greater need for all eyes to be open and accepting of what you fear will bring you down... for the fear of something uncomfortable will turn on you faster than the actual source of the fear itself...

You might want to think about why the fear comes to you... why you allow it to become an obstacle in your day... perhaps it would be a kinder thing for you to do if you recognized that your fear makes you feel negative and begin to work with it... around it... above and below it.. so that one day you will be able to neutralize anything that is uncomfortable for you... as it will have been merged into your more positive thoughts bringing you the peace and the balance you will need in your travels...

It is a big... wide... wonderful world... and it is all yours to explore and learn from and embrace... for truly love abounds in every village... town... city and country... as many of the people themselves hold dear those things that you embrace as well... and look to others... like themselves... for confirmation... as you do...

Truly it is not the people who are the fear mongers... it is more that their leaders have held their place in their societies for so long... resulting in those who chose to live in a world of one-sided thinking and false hope that changes will take place... allowing those in power to remain for long periods of time...

As we said before... it is a wonderful thing to live in the light and want others to do so with you... yet the need for information and understanding that information and working with that as well.. will bring to you a life filled with all things... perfect and imperfect... that you will feel more comfortable living in... and not be a party to reacting to an action that you never really wanted to notice or paid enough attention to... and as a result will seem easier to be part of the reaction to an action than be the action itself... consistently... with very little unexpected reaction...

We are here truly to bring to you the peace and comfort you desire... as we understand the world today is a difficult place to live in and becoming more difficult each day... and only want to see you live in your world in a less worrisome way... for we are with you always... with the love and understanding of who you are and all that you aspire to...

JANUARY 16

We are here truly out of love and concern for the welfare of all mankind... we ourselves have fallen victim to the many years of natural plagues as well as those who were abusers... whether it be governed by political leaders who abandoned the beliefs of fairness and equality of those who believed that no matter what they do... their god will forgive them... we have been held hostage in our own villages... made to withstand starvation and dishonor... and even banishment... through the centuries of persecution... we learned much in the way of forgiveness for those who could not truly understand their wrongs... in a sense we became our own victims... for we knew not to attack our attackers and instead felt the only way was to learn to live within the realm of whatever peace we could find... and in doing so developed a strength that burned strongly within us... and from within us... around us... as the spark within us reached out to all... even our persecutors... and they began to tire... until there was quietness in the land... and to a certain degree an acceptance of our being who we were... we looked towards our peacefulness within for many years... until we no longer were the enemy to those in power... and instead became the ones that were sent to counsel... for even the leaders began to tire of the bloodshed... and began to realize unless they changed... nothing would bring to them a more comfortable life... and so the pendulum began to shift to the other side... and lasted many years...

although there was peace in our land for so long a time... the elders of those times would speak to each generation born of those times before their birth where there was no harmony and little joy... and to know that those times may one day return again... and that it would be our responsibility to quell that powerful force through care and concern and love... not only for our people... yes... we felt that as we would support and soothe ourselves in any way we could... so must we do so for our attackers... and not to spurn them... like a thorn in their side... so that they will continue no longer to bring despair... and instead feel the goodness of spirit in their hearts and minds as well... it is with this thought that we share this writing in this way... for all to understand that with concentrated effort... love will trump hate... for hatred is embedded in those who have experienced the very deeds they try to inflict on others... and many tines... knew only those things... never experiencing love on any level... we worked towards understanding that their hatred in a sense... was a way of justifying their own insecurities... shading them in a sense so that they may not see them or feel them by lashing out... at the expense of others... to shield their vulnerability...

yes... in a sense it all boils down to opening that door to your own vulnerability... feeling the helplessness.. and yet when you begin to feel your inner spark glowing strongly and emanating outward so that others may feel you... it will bring to you the highest level of peace you can experience... filled with happiness and joy... in the many little things as well as the big... for love for yourself holds the highest value of living in the material world... allowing you to sense everything in a different way that you were taught… it is more a deeply internal awareness that brings to you volumes of information for your own welfare as well as the betterment of all mankind…

you are all connected in the material world… and we are all connected in the parallel world and you have aptly named us universal consciousness… be that as it may… we are always present in your physical life… just ask and we shall answer… just think of us and somehow you will begin to feel we are around you… for we are with always, with love and concern for your well-being…

JANUARY 23

How do you measure success... is it luck that helps you to attain what you desire... is it your efforts that make all that you desire happen... is it destiny... and if so... do you believe that you have a destiny in the material world... to attain whatever your destined path takes you... of course... it is not only how you attain that which was designed for you... do you go about it consciously or semi-consciously or unconsciously... and how do you feel when you arrive at that point of recognizing that this was where you were supposed to be... does it feel comfortable for you... and if not... do you feel that there is a need for you to carry yourself through the uncomfortable moments knowing that what is waiting for you will bring you to a better place... and once you were able to withstand the difficulty of getting there... do you feel that this step was just the first of many designed for your growth and greater awareness of all things... soothing your emotions as you begin to open to the many choices you have in life... filled with the adventure if you will... of all things you may have not experienced before... and learning to trust that each step was just the first of many designed for your growth and greater awareness of all things...

for it is actually as if you are being driven by spirit to points of a different kind of reality... one that will open to you like a rosebud... filled with many layers... and learning to allow each layer to open that will correspond to the next step... little by little building in you a greater desire to want to continue to view and feel the dynamics that each layer will offer... knowing that spirit only wants for you to have the emotional freedom to allow yourself to explore without worry... without guilt... as some of those explorations may go into a range of things you were taught not to respect or follow... you will learn to allow your feelings to guide you in ways that you had not allowed yourself to do...

once you begin to open to the nuances of your feelings... and remove your awareness from living only in your everyday practical ego mind... you will begin to flourish as you enter and learn to desire all things coming from that spark that burns like a candle within... never turning off... always bright and alive as it shines with what is for your highest good... and as you begin to work with your spark... the effort will become less and less... until there is no longer any effort at all... for you and your spark... that part of you that lives in your higher self... will have coupled in a way that will no longer feel like a separation... and life will begin to flow as a beautiful river or stream with no rocks... no obstacles... just flowing smoothly towards the direction it was designed to go...

in the beginning as you work this way... you will feel the difference and notice it more and more as you allow yourself to open that door wider and wider... until there is no longer a door... just a passageway... spiritually lit up for you to take your steps... eventually you won't even notice there is a contrast... it will all become parts of the oneness... there will be a melding for the greater good of all that you are and all that you will continue to be as you explore with greater desire those parts of you that you never even knew you had... and welcome each and every day of your life with the joy and the knowing that there will be challenges... and that those challenges will take you to a higher plane... one that you can stand on with confidence and greater interest as you begin to grow into your higher senses... always wanting to reach out for more as you realize that it will be never ending...

for as you grow and reach those higher levels of awareness... so will you bring to yourself those who will bring to you the peace and balance in all things... and in your growth you will have a greater desire to pay it forward... all that you have experienced and all that you embrace will now become what you may offer to others... near and far.. as you begin to understand that you are a part of a much larger circle... connecting from the material world to the spiritual world... always knowing that we are with you always with love and support for your growth materially and eternally...

JANUARY 30

The shape of things today... what are we speaking of...
is it the world at large or small... is it this day.... Is it
one thing you planned to do this day... is it something
you desire... is it something you want to give away... is
it something you fear... or something you adore...
would you rather keep everything in your life as it is this
moment... or are there things you wish you could
change... and would that be for the better or the worse...
if everything stayed the way it is on this day... would
that make you more comfortable and bring you peace...
and if so... do you think changes in your day would
interrupt your peace...

do you not think it may be the telescope you view your
world through... perhaps you may want to open the lens
just a bit at a time so that you may see not only what is
in front of you... you may see what is on the sides of
you and behind you as well as above you... so that you
may understand the bigger picture and the reactions to
just what you see in your small lens that occur all around
you... above and below you...

life is like a kaleidoscope... filled with colors and
motion... it is only still when you do not turn it one way
or the other forcing things to change... so as you can
see... it is your choice as to how you want to view your

world... for if there is no movement... whether it be physical or mental... things will seemingly feel the same... yet there is an action that persists every minute of every day... designed to perform the reaction to an action that takes place... and you may never see it... just know it is happening at all times...

at this point... do you feel more comfortable where you stand in your day... in addition to those thoughts you might have on the subject... you may want to add that whether you move or not... in any direction in your mind or body... know that everything else around you is in its own field of movement... and you may begin to feel out of sync... and ultimately uncomfortable... as you become an obstacle to yourself... not allowing the energy to flow smoothly around you or through you... you may not feel the urge to move in your world... yet you will feel you should and not understand why...

as a material being... motion and change is a way of living so that you may continuously develop your senses... your ideas... your desires... for to remain motionless in a world of motion... only defeats your purpose for being here... motion keeps your body and mind tuned in to all things... and encourages you to want to do more... to reach out to those things that at one time felt distant... and bring them close... allowing them to become part of your routine or... part of your life... and begin to feel comfortable more often than not with those new and different things that enter your life... each and every day... whether it be a surprise or a disappointment... they are there... for your growth and awareness... letting you know that you are not alone in your world... and that there is more to see and feel in your world than you had known existed...

and that is what connects you to all material beings... that desire to be a part of something bigger than yourself... and not believe that you and you alone exist... as you will begin to feel the joy and the sorrow of life in the material world... ever changing and always there... in the state of all things... today... tomorrow and eternally... and remember... that as you begin to move and welcome all things into your world... the challenges and the joy... you will begin to feel things in a different way... as you begin to cherish those things you once took for granted... and will begin to embrace all things as you will know that all things are a part of your life... not for a day... a month or a year... they are forever happening and will continue to do so in the material world and in the spirit world...

in our world... there will be an adjustment in how quickly you move... for in spirit we move rather quickly... more quickly than you do in your material body... yet know that movement is constant and we embrace it as we bring to you... all those around you and those in the world... the love and respect for who you are... as individuals as well as the many groups or factions that you live within... for we are with you always... with love and adoration for all that you are and all that you aspire...

FEBRUARY 7

It would be a far far better world to live in... if you were able to trust in yourselves... deeply trust in the knowing... that what you are doing today is what you were destined to do at this time in the material world... for plans can be made... only to soothe the ego mind... as you all know that many of your plans were never real... they were always subject to change... based on the big picture... your big picture... the plans you made were designed to comfort you... to give you the security blanket you all work under... and yet the true security you will begin to feel is when you live without a security blanket... and allow the knowing to permeate your environment in all ways...

those that can do this... are doing this... they are living with that higher awareness each and every day of their lives... allowing their day to be designed as it should be... each step taken... bringing them to the places and projects that were designed for them to do in their day... and within those projects for their day... it became easier and easier to create that security blanket of calm and balance... for there was no hesitation... no thought... nothing to ponder as a question or doubt as to what or what not they should be doing... those who are still seeking that rapture of peace and balance in their day... contend with the ongoing ups and downs... stalling out and speeding up... being late or being early… as they continue to try to control the outcome of their day…

we are not saying you should not have an outline relating to scheduling your day… as we understand there is a daily projection of what you need to spend where and for how long… what we are saying is… the more you allow yourself to tap into your higher awareness… that place where you instinctively know things… you will never be thrown off when those little things… that annoy you… occur… and know they are going to occur… allowing them to occur with ease and comfort… for they were truly meant to happen in that way… for instance… if you planned something yesterday and were not able to achieve it… somehow if it was supposed to happen… it would happen at a different time on that day or even the next day…

for the many pieces of your big puzzle on your destined path… are laid out for you to see… for you to feel… it is all there… once you reach out and tap into seeing the bigger picture each and every day of your life… the pieces will begin to become more clear as they slowly begin to move closer together… allowing yourself to see them.. it may come in the form of a thought… another person who may say something confirming what you have thought about… it may come as a sound or making a noise signaling something to you… whether it's beware and stop doing what you are doing or begin to do what you need to do… it may come as a feather falling from the sky from a bird's body as it flies over your head… reminding you of something someone once told you… it may come as an offering of peaceful connection with a person who you were warring with and it no longer is meant to be that way… it may come as an animal or a person you meet… in a unique situation where you never expected to meet them… bringing to you an answer to something you were pondering way back in your thoughts and bringing it to the surface... or that person may come into your life to be your teacher for a short period of time... just long enough for you to begin to understand you needed to learn that special something you have been avoiding for so long...

it is preposterous not to think these things can happen... yet they happen each and every day of your life... and you never view them... even from a distance... for you have not yet opened that door of truth... your inner door of trust that lives within you... brought to you by spirit for use in everything that is for your highest good... it is all there... available to you at any given time... all you need to do is to trust yourself... trust that part of you that brings you the answers... even though you may not want them... that brings you the deepest of love... from all those around you in spirit... that harbors no ill will... and only love for who you are...

what we are saying simply... is trust yourself... trust that if things do not happen in the precise order you intended... that they were not meant to happen in that way... and that perhaps it was for you to know that things can happen in all different kinds of ways... and not one particular one... which is usually one of the bigger lessons most of you in the material world hold dear... and that change is not necessarily chaos... and that even in chaos... the truth will stand out in front of it all... to let you know... you are doing exactly what you are supposed to be doing... in the exact place you are supposed to be... and at the exact time you were really supposed to be doing it...

try to let your need for control go... release it into the universe... and allow yourself to be surrounded by your own field of spiritual energy... filled with love and admiration for all that you are... and all that they can help you to be... it will be your truest adventure...

FEBRUARY 13

We shall speak today about our love for all people... all material beings... we have always expressed how we appreciate and respect where you all are in your lives at this time... your burdens and your joy... your laughter and your sorrow... your strengths... your weaknesses... and your desire to connect to your parallel world and finding it to be a struggle... we feel your frustration... and for many... your driving force to sustain a higher quality of life... for those who feel they want to rise above the rest and achieve greater glory...

all this begins with your awareness that you have the seed within you that will begin to grow upward and outward as the light from within begins to illuminate who you are... once you connect to the knowing... your aura field will begin to pulsate brighter and stronger... with a light field of its own color... once you acknowledge that you are ready to connect with yourself on a higher plane of awareness... it is all within you... that ability to know the many things you always wanted to know... and to carry that knowledge with you each and every day of your life... quietly addressing your daily issues with that knowledge within you... so that chaos becomes just another part of your day... and not a drama in your life...

for the more you understand and feel comfortable with the knowing… on a consistent basis… the easier and more comfortable all that will come to you will be… you will begin to start connecting with those many spirit people who have once lived as material beings… in many different aspects of your life… you may draw in those that will help you in your daily struggles to bring joy and balance… and when we say joy… we mean that once you acknowledge those that are around you… you yourself will begin to feel a peace that you never felt before… as their energy will pervade and prevail all of your senses… helping to carry you through the heaviness of your day… without feeling heavy… without the struggle or pessimism that you usually would carry with you… and in fact in many cases… you may feel no stress at all… accepting your day as if your chaos was just part of the day… and focus more on the parts of the day that you will begin to see as beautiful and welcome what you had never noticed before…

there will then be those in spirit who will help to guide you towards what is best for you… what is important for you to know… and experience… who will help you to tap into your inner strengths… your gifts if you will… and to focus on those things… more than the chaos or anything else that is disturbing you in your day… there will be those who help you to develop your gifts… your talents if you will… bringing them out into the light for all to see… and as you do this… each and every day of your life will begin to unfold as the blossoming of a flower… in layers… one at a time… slowly so that you may savor each and every moment… knowing that this was what you were supposed to be doing… and allowing yourself to leave the rest behind…

and those in spirit will begin to surround you with their love as you are beginning to feel their connection… and respect for who you are... and all that you want to be... and will be with you every step of the way... we... collectively are always available and have only the best of intentions for all things that are for your greater good... most importantly... your feelings of well-being... taking the struggle out of the picture... so that more positive things will have the space to take its place... and little by little... your puzzle... your own big picture if you will... will begin to show itself...

suddenly you will begin to get it... to feel it... to adore it... and on your own will want to live within it... in a way you have never lived before... we are happy to feel your energy rising... we are happy to see that you are comfortable with connecting in this way... we are happy to know that you are growing... step by step... towards your dedicated paths and are no longer questioning... or fearful of walking your paths... as you now are aware that you have connected to the knowing...

you are feeling comfortable tapping into this higher consciousness... we say universal... as it incorporates all peoples in all places on the earth who once lived in the material world... you may think of us as each one being its own exclusive volume in an encyclopedia of sorts... waiting for you to open each page that you may need to learn from or answer your questions... we are with you forever... both materially and eternally... and look forward to working with you now... at this time in your life... bringing to you whatever is for your highest good... with love and great affection for who you are...

FEBRUARY 20

We are here with you today to discuss the world's political situation at the hands of those leaders who... in many countries... are not leading with the best of intentions for their people... and because they lead with their ego mind... are producing distorted information and fragile citizenry... for most who live under the domain of those leaders who think of themselves first and their people second... there is a feeling that things are not working as they should and that the people are very limited in their ability to make change... for they elected those who are their leaders... and in some countries did not even have that choice...

these countries that are waging war on others are not paying attention to what needs to be done in their own country for the betterment of their own people... and are in a sense holding their people hostage... not allowing them to be the focus... only the receiver of a fragile foundation... disorganization... doubt and fear... leading to a lack of morals and motivation to want to be productive... and prosper... we feel the heaviness in your world today... for we have experienced similar times... ultimately filled with bloodshed and tears and sorrow... yet we knew that in time the pendulum would swing in the opposite direction and peace would prevail again... at what price... it did not matter... for the damage had been done... and the rebuilding of lives... property and support for one another would once again begin to prevail...

we have seen these senseless scenes many times through the centuries... and how the motivation to succeed shifts back and forth from the citizenry to their leaders and back again... for when there is a lack of motivation to want to be productive and move forward... there will need to be a path you can see or feel that guides you to your place of ease and comfort and you will know you have arrived at what you have worked so hard and so long to get to... if that path is not open to you... motivation is lost... placed far behind your everyday needs of striving to survive... eking out a job here and there... trying to earn a few coins to buy a meal for your family...

for many... everything seems upside down... not real... as if you are living someone else's life... not yours... as you think of how this could all happen... how could your world turn upside down in front of you... as you are living within it... and you feel that you let it happen... even though... deep within... you know you did not have the ability to make the changes necessary to counter the frenzy that your country is now living in...

all of it is unjust... unfair... yet we want you to know that as human beings there is a greater desire for peace than there is for war... there is a deeper desire to share with one another than to take away... to put people into a position of despair... and that the pendulum will only sit in one position from either side of the center for only so long... and will begin to swing towards the center again or the other side... it is extreme either way it swings... for the center is where you want to be... as the center holds the balance that is needed to organize a more efficient and acceptable government... that will hold its people dear to them allowing them to prosper within their regions through peace and tranquility...

you are at a precipice in your lives today... where great change will take place... many changes in fact... some will be desired and some will not be acceptable to all... for everyone has their own needs and will see only what is good for them... and then there will be others who will see what will be good for all mankind...

this is a time in your history where a greater amount of people are opening their eyes and ears to see and hear not only what they want to hear... they are beginning to notice that they have the power to make change... accepting that all change will not be perfect for all... and hopefully will be able to accept that the changes that are made... are for the betterment of all those who perhaps did not have as good a life as they had and will now be on more equal ground...

yes... this is a time of powerful people... in all lands... near and far... who are blustering their way through their lands... with great upheaval... as they are doing what they see fit to do... for what they feel is for the betterment of their people... or not... it is for you to decide... rest assured... these moments will be repeated... until the people begin to gather and make known their feelings and their needs not only for themselves... for all peoples of all lands... for you no longer live on an island unto yourselves...

you are part of the great community of all mankind... easily connected by your transportation vehicles... and may see that what happens in one part of your world... near or far... yet you are all living on one massive material where no matter what happens in any part of your world... the earth will always continue to turn itself completely every 24 hours... as it brings the daylight to you as well as the night... nothing will interrupt that... that is your one given...

MARCH 5

We are the teachers of the universe... we are here to guide you... at times gently nudge you and at other times silent ourselves when necessary... we are the keepers of all information... as we have experienced all information... living within in one way or the other... whether it be on a mental... physical or emotional level... and lovingly desire to share all that we have experienced in the easiest way for each of you to receive it... and put it to its best use... for you and all those around you...

how we bring this information changes with each one of you... for each one of you vibrates on your own individual level... some of you vibrate on a faster or slower level than others... some of you may receive answers to your thoughts within seconds... and others may have to prepare to receive the information in their own individual way... such as prayer or meditation... so that we may transmit to you more comfortably...

still others who receive the knowing may not always be aware in a direct manner that the information is being given to you... for it may come to you in a dreamlike state while asleep or even in your own semi-conscious euphoric zone that you may settle into at times...

still others receive in a very different form than most as they are not of average mind or body... and do not think or act like the average material being... we consider them special beings... and bring them their information in a different way than most... and because of their physical or mental sensitivities... they receive the information even though they may not be consciously aware of it...

then there are those we call sensitives'... who are like an open channel on a radio... or on your computers... when they tune in... it can be almost instantaneous... for their vibration is in a ready state anytime they choose... for them... it is an easier state of mind as they are the believers... and trust in what they receive as they can feel where the information is coming from...

as you work with us more often... it will become that way for you... your body will begin to transition into a receiver... allowing us to bring to you the information more easily... more fluidly... and with less anticipation on your part... how we work with you depends on your own skills... abilities... professions... jobs... talents... and a list of smaller details... for the more we pick up from you and all that you are... the easier it is for us to make the choices of how we want to present the material to you...

if you are a creative person... such as an artist of canvas drawings... we may bring you messages to help you create the picture in a way that you will see things you never paid attention to before... once we understand your skills... we may help to direct you to something you may have always wanted to do and never tried because of your own insecurities... and yet we feel that you have the ability and gently bring to you what you may need to move you forward... so that you may become more productive... whatever your profession may be... we will bring to you the words in the language of your profession... so that it may feel comfortable to you...

yes we come to you in all levels of communication... information is brought to you in all ways... for our desire is for you to feel as comfortable as possible... so that you may continue to work with us for your highest good and share your wealth of knowledge... the physicalities of how we achieve this... differ in each and every one of you...

for some it may be in your dreams... or taking a stroll and beginning to notice that you are not paying attention to anything as you have begun to zone into the knowing... it is easier for us to come to you when you are most comfortable and have an uncluttered mind... which we understand is difficult to do when you are awake... hence the dream work... yet we are with you always... and enjoy working with you whether you are awake or asleep...

and as we said... for some it is easier for you to connect when you meditate... as you begin to bring your mind into the moment with no other thoughts taking up space... allowing the vibration to be more steady with no mental or emotional blockage... allowing the pattern of the vibration to run more smoothly... during meditation... you may feel different things on a physical level just before you go into that higher zone... you may feel fuzzy... you may feel prickly...you may feel as if you are being wrapped in a large cotton ball so that you can hear nothing and see nothing... just feel the words coming through... when you come out of your meditation you may feel as if you have been asleep... and want to stay still for a time... as your heart and other organs in your body have been working more slowly than when you are not working with us...

for or some you may feel heady or dizzy and may need to drink an acidic juice... as to how you begin to connect... for some in the beginning... you may see pulses of colors... pulsing almost like your heart... or fading in and out... each color staying with you for a moment or two... and then changing to another color... for some you may see colors begin to form into shapes... and these shapes may pulsate or float across your line of internal vision... for some... you may see symbols of different kinds that would mean something to you in your personal life... for some you may begin to see yourself in a place that you always felt comfortable in... such as a beach... a waterfall... a forest... flying above the earth... and as you continue to do the work with us... you will begin to be visited by a messenger... whether it be a child or an adult who will take you with them on a journey designed for you only to see... and feel and perhaps hear... and even smell... we work with you in small steps... so that your mind and body will be comfortable... and you will enjoy the time you spend with us... without anxiety or doubt... and as time goes by... each time you begin to connect it will become easier and faster to reach that point of knowing you are working with us... and as your vibration begins to move more quickly... it will be easier for us to meet with you... as we have to slow our vibration down to meet with yours...

we always look forward to working with each and every one of you as we know you are all able and subconsciously ready to connect... we are always available when the time comes that you want to connect... and we are delighted when you do so... our greatest desire is your peace and balance as you live your life in the material world... and that you will begin to feel that way as we work together to bring to you what is for your highest good...

as energies who have lived in your world... we understand your world... and all that it takes to live in it... we also understand our world that we presently live in... and want to share with you all that we... as a collection of groups... can bring to you... knowing that what we bring to you... will feel so comfortable and will last for a period of time... you will want to share all that you feel with the others around you... ultimately bringing harmony through wisdom to all...

MARCH 12

Have you ever thought about how people bracket their words... brackets feel a little stronger than parenthesis... what mood would you be in to put brackets around something as opposed to a softer parenthesis... which could feel like a hug as opposed to a tighter grip...

have you ever thought that perhaps you wear your feelings with emotional brackets on either side of you or in front or behind you... to protect you from receiving feelings or exhibiting your own feelings... as you perceive that those feelings might be painful... and uncomfortable... yet feelings come in all sizes ... and as a result of all circumstances... a laugh or a smile can come from something you are watching or something another person has said to you or perhaps a book you are reading... the urge to hold someone's hand while you are walking or hug someone you care for and are happy to see... or perhaps the satisfaction that you have created something wonderful for another person in their life...

brackets come in all sizes too... some are large enough to cover your entire space that you live in... not allowing other people to enter... others may come in smaller packages and hang around you for only so long or as much as you noticeably need them... some of you might think brackets are a way of supporting yourselves... of holding you together when things around you are falling apart... yet truly brackets are your own device to actually close you off... mentally... physically... emotionally... so that you cannot progress... be productive or feel the joy and peace that comes from integrating your thoughts with others... and from those thoughts allowing your feelings to come to the surface... embracing them with the awareness that as a material being... you need your feelings to be a part of your everyday existence... to bring functionality into your life...

for feelings are the essence of who you are... they drive you one way or the other... and the other is not necessarily wrong... it is more a tool for you to understand and appreciate what you might feel is uncomfortable... feelings are your greatest guide that leads you to your own knowing... your own inner awareness that keeps you on your path... they are the true answer to all of your questions... they are part of who you are... part of your identity... once you can begin to appreciate all that feelings can bring to you... you will no longer even think about the brackets ... and perhaps seldom even use the parenthesis... for you won't need a buffer any longer...

as once you are tuned into your feelings... life will bring you endless possibilities... and we will always be with you... to support you in all your endeavors... as you become more determined to travel on your path of destiny... enriching all the lives around you... as well as your own...

MARCH 19

Break out.... break out from your bonds... those bonds of fixed thinking... and allow yourself to go to that place that fills you with a sense of knowing that you are in that place of comfort in your own thoughts... a place where you no longer have to be concerned about what others think... as you may no longer fall into that abyss of serving others mentally... physically and emotionally... with only what they desire or they think is the right thing for you to think... or do... or not do...

there comes a time in each and every one of your lives where you begin to feel the stirring of emotional disorder... we will call it disorder in that you will begin to feel as if you are being pulled from the group of thoughts you have held on to for so long... as you were taught to do... it is not a good thing or a bad thing... it is what as children.. you were given... to keep you in the family fold and what they felt was traditional thinking... most likely based on their parents traditional thinking... and the generations before them...

we are not saying your biography has been a bad thing... we are trying to point out to you that part of what you have lived with will continue to serve you... and other parts will leave you as you bring in those newer and different thoughts... for the vibration of these new thoughts will stir some of the old ones away... as you will begin to feel somewhat uncomfortable in your old ways of thinking... and there is only so much space for you to hold all these thoughts...

there are many reason for these thoughts to be noticed... you may suddenly feel out of the clear blue... that your mind drifts away from the norm it has been living in... and begins to question what your belief system has always been... and that is the start of a new path you will want to walk on...

slowly... very slowly... you may begin to search for answers you never even had questions about before... you may meet and talk with people who are of a different thought process... in that they are open to challenging their minds with new sparks of light thinking... a thinking of higher awareness... where suddenly you feel as if you would like to connect with those who have crossed and don't know how... you may begin to seek out the books or the places of worship or visit spiritual places on the earth to get a sense of what you are feeling and why...

and yet... what we truly want you to know is that all you need to look for is within you... go within and ask... and you shall get your answers... and your connections... whether it be new friends in the material world or those who have crossed over... for once you begin to allow yourself to open to the changing of your mind... and allow yourself to feel happy about thinking those thoughts... and not doubting yourself or feeling fearful... spirit will begin to connect with you in very simple ways...

it may be where you've had a conversation with other people... and suddenly out of the blue a stranger may come up to you and make the same statements you just discussed… which can be a way that spirit confirms that they are around you… or a telephone may ring and there will be no one on the other end except perhaps static… and suddenly you may think of your friend or relative who has crossed over… you may be thinking of something you wanted… and for some strange reason… you suddenly see it or buy it or it is given to you… for spirit hears you all the time… spirit is as close to you as you are to yourself…

spirit can be the many that are with you every day… coming in and out at will… or those that are brought to you through your own thoughts and questions to help you to feel comfortable and confirm to you that they are there… they will come to you in ways that are compatible with who you are and what you can accept… and suddenly a whole new world will appear before you… and you will suddenly be living with wonder and awe as you begin to realize there is so much out there for you to explore and expand as you open your mind… to reach out for the answers to your questions that you didn't have and now know you need to ask… so that you may begin to feel that connection to what you have been disconnected from for so long…

we will help you at any time… just ask the question and leave that mental door open and we will come through with love and respect for your desire to become part of the knowing…

APRIL 16

There are places in the world today... where most of the people are feeling a disconnect between their leaders... their government... their systems of learning... and are confused and uneasy... not understanding the reason for their feelings...

they continue to plod through their day... day after day... going through the motions of trying to eke out a living to care for their families... they have stopped being concerned about what goes on around them and are only interested in their day to day lives and the sustenance they can bring to their families... and so apathy has appeared causing a very big separation from their bigger picture...

for they no longer feel that they are a part of their world... since their leaders seemingly ignore their ideas... their concerns and their circumstances in which they live... and so government has become even bigger and broader and its tentacles have begun to reach out to all those who no longer care and tell them what they need to care about instead...

the future of today has already become altered... little by little... the pieces of the puzzle no longer join in the direction they once were... and because of that... the people are feeling frustrated and feel less trust for those they once honored for their opinion... and once that mistrust begins to grow... there is a feeling of disconnection from all they have lived with in their comfort zone of how life was and thought it would continue to be... adding to their uneasiness each and every day... worry has begun to rear its head and have made them feel less productive as they now see that no matter what they do... nothing seems to change...

spirit sees this and wants to let them know that they are around them at all times... spirit wants them to feel that they can ask any question or share their concerns and spirit will help them to feel more at peace... for spirit has been through these issues of today many times through the centuries and understands that this too shall pass... the pendulum will begin to swing to the other side in time... as nothing stays the same forever...

it is our desire to share with you all that we hold true so that you once again feel that you can make change... and perhaps not only you... for you can bring your thoughts and hopes and dreams for your future to all those around you who may feel the same way... and together as a large unit begin to once again voice your opinions and arouse those who have been living listlessly and discordantly to once again become interested in their lives... where they will begin to feel that they count...

each and every one of you can make your own big picture in a puzzle of many pieces... fitting together in perfect harmony for all to see and hear... and will continue to grow in number as you become a united front for what you were meant to have... peace and tranquility in your world... in your country... in your home... and will look forward to getting up in the morning... knowing that you are now a part of a very important day as you are going to be a part of your future... today and each day to come... feeling the light of a brighter future as we are with you always... with love and great concern for you and for all those who live in the material world...

APRIL 30

Do not blush when people compliment you... do not make excuses... do not question why you received their compliment... let it be... feel it... embrace it... for you are embracing yourself with what another person saw or felt in you... and wanted to express that feeling they received when they were near you... it may not always be obvious what another person sees in you... for many times you may have to stand in a mirror to try to sense why it is that other people compliment you... as you may not always understand it at that time...

does this phenomenon exist for so many... yes... we see the beauty of your soul in all of you... and are happy that you are given the opportunity to know it exists when other people see it too... as for the many... your day is filled with all the pinning's of the necessary things that are either required of you or you choose to do... that have nothing to do with getting to know your inner beauty... that part of you that radiates from within...

you go about filling your day with the number of things you feel you must do... and are satisfied that you completed your list... never taking that moment in time to touch what has been within you all the time... your spiritual connection... that essence of thought and feeling on a higher level than your everyday life allows... for we agree... that everyday living in the material world is heavy... and not always supportive...

we are always trying to bring to you the ability to reach for what is within and hold it in front of you as if looking in a mirror... unveiling what you have carried with you all your life... that spark that shines within you bringing to you the comfort... contentment... balance and love for all things... ready and waiting for you to acknowledge all that exists within... and patiently waiting for you to come to terms with it...

as you begin to do when people compliment you... accepting that the beauty within you is as important or more important than the beauty on the outside of you... and that you will be able to appreciate and cherish that which is most important... the ability to love... unconditionally... without expectation... all those you hold close to you... and that you will want to be available to share your inner beauty with whomever may need you to be there for them... and as you make those connections... you will be allowing them to open into their own higher self as they connect with you... and all those around them...

and the network will continue outward... widening the big picture of your life... as you connect with the many in their lives... it will be a beautiful flow chart of loving energy... soothing the savage beast as they say... bringing a higher awareness so that people will begin to live in peace... knowing and feeling that higher place they can go to for love... to go to for a sense of feeling safe and secure within themselves... to go to that place where they will begin to understand that they are just part of the picture... and want to step into the other pictures of those around them... so that they can feel what others feel... and because of that ability... understand more what their responsibilities are in their own world and the worlds beyond them...

MAY 21

Begone cruelty... begone pain... begone suicide... begone divorce... begone poverty... begone tyranny... begone the despair that comes from feeling isolated... whether it is in the immediate family or by those holding the people of tribes or small towns or countries hostage... for fear that they will break out from their emotional and physical bonds and change the emotional or political environment...

for those who feel all those frustrations deep into their soul will continue to feel helpless and feel that no one else cares about them... and ultimately feel their life has no meaning... unless they can do something... anything would feel better than nothing... any little change... even if they could just get up one morning and feel blessed that they are still alive... and from that day forward bring that feeling to the others in their tribes... their villages... their towns...

and as those feelings begin to spread... they will feel that life... no matter how poor in every area it is... still has a richness to it... as you watch the drama unfold each and every day... you also begin to notice that your baby is beginning to walk and another child has picked up some stones and is throwing them at a circle on a tree... playing his own game... for the material being is a beautifully complex body made of an intricate structure designed for you to survive... no matter what the abuse... it is rigid in its thinking that you must live... and within that thinking is the hope that life will get better... for without hope the human body will shut down...

hope is what can be spread amongst the thousands who feel that one day their freedom will come... whether it is through leaving their place of birth or gathering together in their masses to overtake their leaders... to appease themselves... many have even started their own groups to discuss in the darkness how they can survive together... helping each other to stay emotionally as well as physically strong until those in the outside world can pay attention to their situation...

and as those small groups begin to develop in their communities... they begin to connect like a network... with their thoughts... hopes and dreams... all coming together for the common good... and suddenly beginning to feel that their words will count... their words can bring attention to their plight... their words are as powerful as those keeping them from growing into developing themselves and all those around them into a society of free people...

they then realize that there are those who will have to speak their words... out into the public... and their leaders will hear their words... and perhaps offer them the peace they so richly deserve... and if not... their hope is that the world around them will begin to notice that their words can become the same words as those around others who think it will never happen to them...

for nothing stays the same... all things shift... some for the greater good... some not... yet once the pendulum swings most can adjust to the changes for it does not swing swiftly... it swings slowly so that you may begin to feel the changes more easily and become aware of your choices... so that once it stops you are already in place... yes... how change affects you boils down to the choices you have and whether or not you make them... for your own good as well as all those around you...

choices are your greatest gifts... for even those who are burdened with most of their human rights taken away from them... still have choices on how they look at life... and finding the things that they hold dearest to be the most important... we are always here to help you to find those choices... be aware of them and that you can go to them... even in the darkest moments to find them and connect with the spirit within you that will bring you the peace and balance you begin to desire... whether you are locked in a physical prison or an invisible one... we are with you always with love and great respect for all you endure each and every day of your lives...

MAY 28

It is a far better thing to know... than not to know... or even to just think about what you would want to know... for even just thinking about something sparks your ability to process the what... when... where and why... questions are better than no questions at all... for questions are the doorway to wanting to know something... that is either triggered by an action or is a reaction to what has occurred...

can you imagine a world where thinking about what you would like to know is not possible... it never occurs... it is not something that is discussed... there are no questions because there is no reason to think about a question... you just accept where it is you are in all things... you don't think about the past or the present... you don't even think about the moment you are in...

you are represented as if you are flattened out like a sign you may see on the roadside advertising a product... a big bold sign that has no life to it other than to be noticed by others... who once they see it go about their day forgetting it... yet there are places in the world today... where each day is the exact same day as the day before and will be like the day after...

the people that live in those parts of the world have no thought about what they would like to eat... drink... sleep in... or walk about... they are self-made prisoners in large self-made villages designed to harbor them from those who are trying to hurt them... the one thing they do feel is that they hold hope close to their hearts... praying each day for those who will help them... in any way possible... they have not given up on themselves... for they know once hope is gone... the light within will extinguish itself...

be aware that there are numerous parts in your world today that have these communities of great numbers of people who travel long distances to safety... living in poverty to survive... one day at a time... with no thought about their choices for they know there are none... and yet the one thing no one can take away from them is their hope... to be free to live in a world where they can visit with others without worrying about physical abuse or murder... where they can talk freely about what they think about without becoming a prisoner... to bring their children into a world of peace and the freedom to think about what they would like to become and feel the pride in actually doing what they had always thought about...

there is strength in thinking... in bringing your thoughts to the forefront and holding them there for as long as possible... to help guide you through your day with great anticipation for the next day to come... it is not that you may feel that to do that is to feel discontent... it is more that to have the ability to think is your connection to your higher self... to aspire to a more evolved human being... to develop your gifts as you think about what you would like to bring to you and all those you hold dear rippling out to the world around you... to think has always been the trigger that opens the doors to all that is out there and available for you to bring into your life… and once acquired to pay it forward to all t those who need to connect to their "thoughts"…

JUNE 4

Warming the heart...where does that come from... does it come from one's words... one's actions or one's feelings... and do you respond to any of these things with your heart... or your mind... or your body... warming the heart is a way of saying how you feel when another person speaks to you... or touches you or just sits quietly next to you... do you think warming your heart comes from another or from you... have you ever sat with another person and when they spoke to you in an angry manner feel warmth in your heart... and do you not feel that this warmth in your heart is coming from you even though they are speaking in a stern manner...

for you have connected with their heart in a more positive way as you don't allow the surface of this person to disturb you... you are connecting directly to their heart... their inner flame... their soul... and as two souls connect with each other on that level... there is truly nothing that can be said that would disturb you or the other if you are equally connected... and even if the two of you are not equally connected... you will both feel an inner quietness calming you down as you sit quietly just sending warmth to each other's heart... as you are able to practice this exercise in soul connection more often than not... you will begin to realize that you do not have to wait until you cross to connect to your higher self...

you can do this very simply while you are in material form... you might want to try the exercises that relate to allowing yourself to be more passive and less resistant to hearing the brutish words... and allow yourself to slip into that place of love and kindness for the other... as you decide to leave your normal reaction behind and begin to feel the warmth of your own heart for the others who may be in great turmoil and do not stop to pause... and take a moment to allow what is uncomfortable to pass... without doubting your thoughts about yourself or the other person... or feeling neglected or neglectful towards the other person...

connecting to another is a system unto itself... for it contains great patience as it becomes more sacred than any material thing you own... it becomes sacred as you begin to understand a way of being in a relationship that offers you greater awareness in all things... for as you take that first step of connecting to another in the simplest of ways... step two will begin to appear and step three and four... and as you live in those steps each day... you will want to drop that part of you that was used as a defense mechanism as it will no longer serve your purpose... you originally designed that behavior as a way of keeping yourself less vulnerable while attempting to make yourself look stronger and smarter than the other person...

what you are beginning to embrace is that your need to feel stronger and smarter comes from a place of peacefulness and quiet... quieting your mind to allow the knowing to permeate your entire being... allowing you to pause as you take that moment in time to recognize that warmth within you that you now desire to share with another... and will come to realize that by doing so... you have enabled another to feel that beautiful connection of love coming from the warming of your hearts...

JUNE 11

It is truly your time for the peoples of the world to lock hands and meditate together... in all your languages... uniting in your thoughts for the changes you know must take place to bring to you all the understanding that even though you are separated by bodies of water and lands that are difficult to live on... you are connected as people with hopes and dreams of a brighter future for yourselves as well as your children and your children's children... and that it is all of your responsibilities to join the cause for what is so important at this time... your freedoms... to choose how you want to live... where you want to live... and peacefully live with your belief systems... even though they differ from others... since life began as you know it... there have been wars... small ones and big ones... and usually not for the cause of the peoples of the land... more for the cause of the leaders of the land... in the world today...

you have the ability... what with your newer communications... to share with the world your problems... and to stand as a single unit against the barbaric control of your leaders... the unit you will form will be communicated out to the world at large... and if you stay your course... will be supported by others who may be just beginning to realize that who they are and how they are living is single minded... for they are also beginning to feel the creation of tyrannical behavior in small ways and yet it is important to know... that nothing can justify what is going on today in the world at large... and nothing is an isolated behavior...

at one time if you did not see or hear the problems in the world... you didn't have to think about them... yet today you are seeing the communications from every part of your world and need to be aware that this too could happen in your own back yard... it is not that farfetched... for the pendulum in the world today has begun to swing and stay in one direction only... unfortunately it is a negative direction that has caused many deaths and will continue to cause more...

yes we know from our own histories that the pendulum will once again move to either a neutral position or a more positive one... but at what sacrifices... and how long do you want those sacrifices to go on... your world... the one you personally live in... needs to make changes... before the energy that has spilled out over the many miles near and far reaches out to touch you... there is very little safe harbor in the world today... we are not trying to sound too negative... we have seen these warring rituals many times over... from the beginning to the end of them... and we understand how it all starts and how it can end...

we are with you to bring to you the truth... in all things... many times the truth is not always what you want to hear or know... yet the truth does not change for any person... place or thing... it is what it is... truth can change to another truth... yet it can never be undone... it stands on its own energy source...

we are bringing this line of thinking today for your education and for you to allow yourself to see all sides of the information you are being given so that you may make your choices as wisely as you can... given the small amount of time you have lived in the material world... mostly it would be to your benefit to feel what you hear and see... and imprint that feeling into your emotional body... for if you only live in the mental... you can sail through anything... and miss many things...

the key here is not to miss anything... for at this time in the world... every bit and piece of information is a treasure... if you can receive communications from all parts of the world... you are luckier than many who cannot... and again we say it is your treasure chest of gold... the information bringing to you the capability to ponder what is for your highest good and your families and friends highest good... and like the ripples in a pond... it is your responsibility to do the right thing... do not ignore what you feel cannot touch you... for that is the biggest falsity... and one you go to as your safety net...

we understand there is a part of you that fears thinking that you could become a victim of tyrannical leaders as other countries have... and yet... as we have said before... many times... that is exactly the way things start... when your belief system fights to protect you from over exposure... it is actually beginning to shut you down... for your own safety and peace of mind... be more accepting of the facts and for your own security... do not dismiss them...

we are not saying you should live with all the negative information you are hearing every minute of every day... we are saying ... when you live in the world... if you want to truly live in your world... you need to be aware of what your world is truly all about... if your first concern is to try and fix it... know that you can begin by gathering those close to you and forming a common bond of integrity for who you all are… and the energy will move forward attracting others of your thought processes… and so it will spill into still others that may… in the beginning… not feel comfortable with you and in time will become compatible with you…

it is all a process… know that once this begins to develop… the pendulum will begin to move… even in its tiniest increments to the other side… away from the negativity and into the knowing… making change in the world for the common good of all mankind… we are here for you always… and if you have questions… we can bring you the answers… just ask

JULY 1

In your world of today... life is expanding in less than the time of a second... and at all times in all places for all reasons... it is a fusion of energy designed and developed by all those who dictate how the world shall live... the need to impact the world of today is no longer designed for one small area of the world... it is more directed outward to blanket the population of the world with what some see as good and others see as bad... for it is the perception of those who can dictate what they feel is best for all... it is a caldron boiling over with anxiety... control... and domination... yes it is filled with what you would call the good and the bad... depending on where you stand in the world today...

there was a time... not long ago... where the world was a melting pot... a welcomed melting pot... for people were beginning to become interested in how not only how they lived... they were interested in how what you would call foreigners lived... and in finding out the things they wanted to know realized that those foreigners were not so foreign to all things they knew... as they realized that people on both sides had differences and they had commonality... they felt the love for their families... and hoped that their children would have a better life than they had... they both fought in wars they were forced to do... they both were led by leaders who felt they were in the right... even though they may not have been...

today the caldron runneth over... filled with the reactions to all those actions that were created in the past... whether good or bad... right or wrong... these reactions exist now... and are at times governed by people of different generations than long ago... yet they stand in the same places in their thinking... what is fair and just to one may not be for another... and so it goes...

we have seen these shifts in power many times over... this kind of world you live in today is similar to many other times where people felt the need for change... and change was brought to them... not necessarily the way they had planned... spirit is working very hard to bring a comfort zone... even a small one and perhaps only for a few moments at a time... to all those who feel lost... abandoned by their leaders... and are crying out for the dignity they feel they deserve... where their input was at one time counted...

once you begin to move on a singular course... productive and progressively towards bringing ideas to the table for peace to thrive once again... it will be the first step towards fulfilling the true changes you all have desired for so long...

it must be done in a peaceful manner and in very large numbers so that you will sway those in power to want to hear your words... for truly... you are their support beneath what they stand for... without you all... there would be nothing ... you may want to think about this... without you... your leaders have no one to lead...

the winds of time are changing the direction of the energy… it is not moving quickly… it is staggered and at some points has stopped and so the energy is like a huge cloud with no wind to push it away… it's just hanging on until your energy… the people in your part of the world… and those in all of their parts of their worlds… come together as a unit and stand firm on moving those dark and heavy and oppressive clouds away into the universe… and allow the light to bring back the vim… vigor and enthusiasm to your day… and all days to come…

we understand this is a big task… one many of you may feel with dread… yet know that it only takes the first step… that very first step to begin the momentum needed to fight the fight through peaceful methods… staying the course knowing it might be a long one… and yet realizing that nothing stands still forever… the energy does not stay in one place forever… everything moves at one time or another… you can be that shifter… the one that inspires all to see a truly better world that will bring peace and balance in all ways for all people today… and for the generations to come…

JULY 8

The energy in the world today feels brutal... blustery and uncomfortable... it has infiltrated families... the dynamics of the families... in a way that is beginning to cause frustration... anxiety and lack of communication... for people are at a loss for words... they feel words will no longer make a difference... they feel their emotions flailing... helplessly trying not to feel the darkness they feel is coming... there is bitterness as well as a feeling of the joy they once had in their lives... when people would come together to share their day... to share their thoughts about their future... and about their children's future...

the future now looks bleak to them... and they struggle with trying to hold their heads high and not feel the heaviness bludgeoning them... they feel as if they had been played... like children... hoping so hard that their dreams would come true... they followed the words of a man they had felt would lead them to a place where life would be more comfortable... less burdensome with more advantages for themselves as well as their children... they listened to his sweet words of connection he seemed to make with them... as if he was listening to their thoughts... hopes and dreams... and turned them into his thoughts... hopes and dreams... they had actually felt exhilarated at times watching him walk with an air of confidence as if he could do anything he wished… and he has…

alas… it is not even close to what they thought it would be… as they thought their lives could be so much better… they would now be pleased if their lives were at least where they were before he began to speak so righteously about the many changes he would direct to help those who had been left behind for so long… it all seemed to make sense at the time… as they wanted him to say the words that they thought were so right… they longed to have a leader that would listen to their voices and lead them to a place of more comfort and security… they wanted these things so badly that they actually did not really hear the words… for their thoughts had colored his words over and over… so that they would think his words were their thoughts… yet they found that his words were twisted and unseemly… they were a pattern of words that were repeated often to imprint what they thought they heard… and thought they understood… and now realize too late that this man was a walking talking mouthpiece… designed entirely for his own plan to change the country in a way that the founders of the country would shake in their boots…

for he has redesigned the laws that were written to protect all the people… to make them fit into his grandiose scheme of changing the direction entirely to fit the changes in the entire way all will live… and yet another struggle will begin to ensue… making the struggles you thought you had… pale by comparison… this writing is not meant to frighten you… more to bring you to a place where you can face your thoughts… and separate them from his thoughts… and bring you back to a time where you could think clearly and concisely about your own world… the community you live in and what you truly desire... and how to achieve what it is you need...

this writing was meant for you to read over and over again... until you see that words can be interpreted by the many in the ways they want you to hear them... it is a process of how the brain functions... you are not to blame... there is no blame here... this writing is to focus on these actions as a course in history... because you have such an open government... the rules are vulnerable... and there have been before and will be again those who are willing to interpret the rules in their own way and make change... over and above what is thought to be best for all people...

this writing is designed for all to be ever watchful... never allowing yourselves again to be satisfied with simple words that seem to make sense... those words that you wanted so much to make sense... and that you will want to read more about those who are saying the words... and not just listen... do your homework as a child does... so that you can learn to make the best choices for yourselves and question... question... question... and not necessarily accept what you are told... and mostly... be vigilant in listening with your feelings... for your feelings never lie... let your feelings be your words... let your feelings talk to you on a level of higher awareness... so that you will once again be able to make the choices that are best for you and your family... all of life in the material world are lessons well learned... and right or wrong... the key to it all... is that you learn from your lessons what to do and not to do for the future... feel the truth... and you will find the answers...

JULY 15

The world today can become a far far better place than it is at this moment in time... it has been foraging through the ravishings of war and discontent for some time now... and is very ready for a change... when we say you are at a precipice and have the ability to swing the pendulum in the other direction... we are saying the swinging of the pendulum is a mindset of sorts... for the minds of most of the populace must all be tuned into the same frequency of thought... to move the energy from where it is to where it truly needs to be...

we can only bring to you the status in the material world at any given time... it is your responsibility to feel what we are saying and allow yourself to understand the feelings you are receiving when you read our words... so that you may shift the energy towards what you are truly feeling and desire... which would ultimately become a momentous occasion... for all in the vastness of your material world... as once the shifting begins here or there... it will ripple out as it continues to balance the changes that have begun to take place... and will continue to do so until it reaches a balance... think of it as a fine tuning fork... set at a certain pitch... when you tap it... it will reverberate until it crosses the distance it takes to reach a balance in the vibration...

your feelings are vibrations... whether they are considered to be bad feelings or good feelings... it is all about the purpose and intention of what you desire for yourself first and then reflect out to the world... the world as you live it in your own community and from there to the next community and from there to the next... will continue to move on as the energy builds upon itself to send the messages of love and peace as far and as long as it has to go until it reaches a balance... and until it does there will be pockets of areas in the world that will still be filled with chaos and strife...

this is not one person's responsibility nor one country's responsibility... it is the responsibility of the world as a whole... united together in the need to connect in peace and love for who you all are... for you all come from the same source... and are made with the same matter... and live upon the earth you share with each other... near or far...

how you dress... what language you speak... what food you eat... what traditions you embrace and not be examined and judged... all these things are like a beautiful array of different kinds of flowers... when you look at the abundance of the flowers in a photograph you begin to see how beautiful all the differences are when they stand together... united in their independence and yet loving the fact that they are all part of the same oneness... and there is no desire to exclude one from the other because they don't match or aren't equal in beauty...

it would be wise to take a lesson from nature... who does not discard... the biggest or smallest... the ugliest or the prettiest... the aggressive or the passive... the hungriest or the fulfilled... everything in nature takes care of itself... the creatures that walk the earth in their large herds from country to country take care of themselves... it is only when humans take it upon themselves to feel they must do something better than nature or the creatures have done... as their ego prevails...

and now man and woman have taken it upon themselves to do what they feel is justice to those they encounter... within the many groups they live and those afar... many years ago... tribes in all cultures... lived amongst themselves in peace... yes there were many wars too... and yet there were many years of peace in between the wars... as they evolved in their emotional development and began to feel the need for peace more than war... they began the conversations of what they needed to do for each other that would allow peace to prevail...

and so it grew from there... a better understanding that wars were not meant to be the best thing for the general populous... only the best thing for the political situation in the world... where power was embraced more than cherishing the love for peace... and so you have gone off-track... off the path of what the original purpose and intent has always been... since the world of Atlantis... where peace prevailed for a very long time...

it is now your responsibility to allow yourselves the ability to work through your discord amongst your own groups... and allow the other groups in the world to work amongst themselves... and as in nature... it will bring balance back into the biggest puzzle of all... so that you may see your place in that big picture...

JULY 29

The world of today... the world of tomorrow... and the world of yesteryear... seek not to be the same... not even to be similar... only to be cautious and balanced... to learn from the past to live in the present and to gift the future with the knowledge of learned lessons...

truly it is not about thinking or comparing what was in the past with today and hoping that things will be better tomorrow... it is your embracing where you are at this moment in time... so that you may elevate yourself from the drudgery of worry... hopelessness... anxiety and an all-around feeling of helplessness...

for it appears that a malaise has begun to cover the world... almost as if an acceptance of what is and what it is going to be... and as you question all those thoughts that come in and out of your scope of awareness... you will continue to stay in those moments... and will continue to live with the anxiety of what is known and what is unknown... all those thoughts that are steadily coming through that truly bring you none of the tools to feel more comfortable in your daily life...

for if each one of you began to look at your day as one of many in a week and your week as one of many in a year... think of all the exploratory things you can add to your schedule that is basically filled with rising from sleep… inhaling a morning's meal… scampering to your field of employment… and to coming home to a daily dinner ending your day with somewhat sleepless nights…

it is a formula for those who will feel less productive and very much accepting that this is all life has to offer… yet when you truly think about what there is around you to connect with… the numbers are great… as you look around… in your place of residence… noticing the landscape as you walk or drive to your job… how things may have changed when you leave your job… all the conversations you have had in a day which may open your eyes to new and interesting things you have never done before… sharing your thoughts in your work environment with the others who may feel they are in the same predicament… begin to enjoy and appreciate the abundance of food sold in your marketplace all laid out for you… instead of looking at it as a chore… for there are many in the world who have never seen markets as large… when you look around your landscape… try to see it as if you were a camera… focusing on a small piece of a tree… a flower an insect… as they are all growing and reproducing… not concerned with outside influences… they are focused… and in their focus they bring balance into their lives… they are not concerned with everything… they focus on one thing at a time… you may want to focus on your pets… and watch how they do what they do… they eat… sleep … play and clean themselves… they also ask attention from you when they need it and are always giving it to you whether you need it or not… their lives are very much in balance… for the most part… of course a long walk in the day would be the cherry on top of a sundae for them…

what we are trying to point out to you... is that life can be very simple... slow it down a bit and it can be more illuminating... speed it up a bit by adding more tasks to it and it becomes busier yet not as illuminating... add more things into your life and it becomes filled with the need to find places to put more things... still not as illuminating...

for illumination comes from within... from allowing yourself to connect to what is truly important around you from within... trying to stay in a moment in time for a small amount of time... perhaps just enough to watch a butterfly flutter its wings as it goes from one place to another... or sit quietly watching children playing in a park... or standing on a pier watching the birds flying over the water as the sun is setting for the day... and you may begin to notice the many other quietly interesting events taking place all around you... whether quietly or loudly... it will fill you with that peace and tranquility you are all grasping for as you speed through your lives filling it with things to help soothe your anxieties...

we understand you all have a need to want to satisfy your yearnings... and may do it in different ways... yet that is only a momentary fix... the true balance will come from the acceptance of all that is around you... both what you name beautiful and ugly... that live with you and around you each and every day... they are your own keys to the kingdom of true happiness... as in those moments where time stops... you will find the contentment needed to achieve the peace that will bring you the knowledge that will make you happy forever...

AUGUST 19

We feel the chaos… the strife and the uncertainty in the world today… we ourselves are more than dedicated to bring you the words that will bring a bit more peace into the hearts of all those who struggle with their day each and every day and their unknown future… for themselves as well as their families and their communities…

yes we understand that it is a harsh world you live in … and it may seem that any gain is at the expense of the many others… yet there are times that to suffer can bring you to a higher awareness as you feel the pain and know that others are feeling the same thing you are… you may understand and feel their passion for the peace the many are struggling to hold…

yes we hear your thoughts of uncertainty… and again we say that many times uncertainty brings you to a higher place within your own thinking where you find that you do not have to succumb to it… you can walk right through it and stand tall at the end… knowing that you have survived the worse and are moving forward to something better…

we hear your thoughts of feeling lost… out of control… needing the structures you have set up for yourselves to prevail… and yet everything seems like it's twisting and turning and sometimes turning upside down before it stands upright again… these are all products of the fear that enters you… relating to the fear of the unknown… the unspecified… the unbalanced … yet there is a classroom of subject matter within you now you never experienced before… demanding you to grow beyond what you thought you could ever do before… teaching you the steps to walk as you masterfully begin to learn that you can do what you think you can… and nothing less…

for once you begin to believe that where you are is not the place you want to be… you begin to want to step outside of your picture and allow yourself to be carried to a space that is unstructured and not familiar… allowing yourself to be guided by your inner knowing… to bring you to that place of higher awareness so that you may build a different structure that will carry you through the muck you are presently living in…

you are starting to develop a burning desire to attain a higher level of awareness so that you can find your peace … a place where there are no expectations… and only acceptance for what comes to you… as you learn to find only the high points that are now vibrating with your higher self… and leaving the rest behind… for even in the ashes of a home burned down… those who have the tenacity and staying power to pursue something that would bring them to that place of comfort… may find a picture frame and if they are lucky even the picture that lived in that frame… so that they may look at it as it brings them fond memories of a wonderful moment in their life that they now can carry with them forever… helping them to gain the strength they need to move forward… productively and with the desire for growth… as they expand in their thinking… and a better connection with all those they have known for so long and never paid attention to…

we understand how difficult your struggles may be… and yet we truly feel that the struggles that you are living through… like the house of ashes… will be imprinted in your mind so that you will carry them with you as a shield against all the negatives… all the difficult paths you may walk and will eventually reach the end as you eventually reach your greatest connection… the connection to your soul… that part of you that has lived with you for so long… always there for you to feel… sense and connect with…

yes… you will begin to feel that greater sense of all that you are as you travel together to reach out to the new world that is out there for you… for all that once was… is no longer comfortable for you as you are no longer that person… like a caterpillar you have begun to shed your form only to emerge as a beautiful being… who is feeling lighter and happier and most appreciative of your awareness to your connection of the knowing…

SEPTEMBER 9

Have you asked yourself why you're here... why you were born into the family you live with... why do you have brothers or sisters or both... or none... do you even wonder about all this at all... and if so... why is it important to you... there are several thoughts in the material world about these things... one thought goes in the direction of scheduling when and where you may live... either for the first time or perhaps the 2nd 3rd or 4th times you have lived as a material being... there are others who feel that there is no choice... that it is an actual physical connection at first between two people... and that once that connection is made... the spark of life enters into the physical body... growing and living within that body for the rest of that person's physical life... leaving to return to its origins only after the body has ceased to live in physical form...

we realize there is a certain anxiety about the who... what... when and where of all this... we feel those points of interest are best left alone at this point in our writings... and perhaps think it would be best for you to examine your thoughts through your process of meditation... and as you quiet your mind asking for guidance... and are truly ready for the answers... we shall try to bring them to you... as we always do... when and if you are ready to hear them...

the question we would like to address at this time is why you are in the physical form today and why it is important for you to know the reason... there are a multitude of reasons why each and every one of you are living in this material form at this time... for we see the world where life is lived in constant chaos and uncertainty... and understand why you would ask yourself why you would want to live in the world of today... what could you benefit from doing so...

we would like you to think about that for a moment... and perhaps may want to change the question to now that I'm here... what can I do to help the world today... how can I as one person do anything to help the world today... I would really like to do something that would make a difference and yet what can one person do... these are the most consciously aware questions that will give you the greatest of answers once you begin to go within and allow yourself to open to the thoughts that will begin to calm your mind and open your heart... for as much as it seems to be an endless tirade of madness... think of it all... knowing that there is a great part of the picture that is coming from your perception... yet even in the darkest of moments... there will always be a pinpoint of light... it will always be there for you to see it... if you allow yourself to see it...

for most... you seem to directed towards the negativity... pessimism and uncertainty... and yet even with all that is surrounding you... there is that little bit of light... we shall call it hope for now... that propels you out there even for a few steps towards seeking that calmness that hope can bring... and learning that if you can venture out even a few steps... you could add a step or two towards the direction you want to take each and every day... building slowly the strength and attention to finding that place in the world where you are supposed to be... and even as one person... can begin to develop the thoughts in your mind that can convert into whatever your gifts may be... that will carry the messages to the world... whether it is your world in your own community... and from there to other communities and to those across your bodies of water to the many others who truly need encouragement... to wake up in the morning and live through their day...

for each day is precious... and as you begin to bring hope to the others around you and they to others around them... life begins to feel more precious... and you begin to feel you are learning your purpose... whatever that may be... for to make a difference one does not have to be a leader of the world... it may be to just validate another person's existence by saying good morning... how are you... I hope you have a nice day... what a gift you brought to them... that will brighten their day and make them feel they count... and as they feel that way... think of how they will encourage the many others they come in contact with... just by them feeling their happiness and joy...

it is and has always been the small things that people forget from day to day and year to year... as they go through their busy schedules and become part of the masses... sometimes all moving at the same time going to the same places... yet we do not want you to lose your individuality... and become invisible... we would like to see the peoples of your world... connecting... even if it is one person at a time... so that eventually the connection that started on your side of the world... will manifest itself to the other... bringing an awareness that you are truly connected... through your blood... sweat and tears to each other... and hopefully will begin to feel that love and respect... creating a higher awareness that will ultimately end the suffering...

and as we started this writing asking why are you here... hopefully those everywhere will feel your presence as you share your wealth of gifts with all those around you... so that the linkage begins to spread across the continent... one person at a time... reconnecting to that person on the other side... we understand this cannot happen on a physical level... yet it is a thought... a very large thought that can persist... if you allow it... so strongly that it will attract others who will attract others... wanting to be a part of that feeling of the knowing... we will continue this writing soon.

SEPTEMBER 23

It is a wide and beautiful world... as you view it from your movie screens... books... pictures... does it not make you wonder how it is you feel safe when you walk through nature's finest forests... parks... the woodland rivers and the magnificent bodies of water... secure and in awe of it all... and when you fly in your planes... does not the earth look peaceful and calm and everything seems to be moving slowly with no need to move quickly as the cars... trains and busses travel from one place to another... and if you had not read your volumes of books that introduce you to other worlds on the earth... that have not yet been seen by your eyes... you would believe what you see as you walk or travel is what life is all about everywhere...

once you begin to be aware of other lands filled with other people... do you not wonder what their lives are like... before your communications made it possible for you to view other lands... did you not think that life where you are is the way life is in distant lands... and yet even though you now know of distant lands and their cultures... what pictures do you view... perhaps happy children dancing in costumes... people selling their food and wares in the streets... peacefully living in their environment... yet it is what you do not see that is most important... for there is a growing number of areas that live with famine and futility... disease and despair... with no hope for change... yes... there are the many who need to be validated and not rejected from society... just because you don't see them...

we understand that this is not a comfortable subject for you to discuss or ponder... and you may even feel that with all you have available... there are people out there who are doing their job of helping those that cannot help themselves... caught between warring factions and the naiveté of others who think all this will get better... that you do not have to do anything...

we are not writing to you today to disturb your peaceful lives... more to bring to you the awareness of those who do not now or have ever had peaceful lives in their own lifetime... and desperately need those that do... to help bring to those who do not... the hope for their future and their children's future... it all begins with helping to educate people in any form available... so that they may think about how others live and begin to know that with the proper support.. they may have choices too...

we know that there are many groups of people who are miraculously struggling to bring to those weary and repressed peoples of the world... some hope and support so that they may know the world knows about them... these are the miracle workers... these are the people who do the hard work... these are the people who need you to not only be aware... be where you can make a difference... in sharing that part of yourself in helping to build a relationship... bonding with those who need you... bringing a special kind of enrichment to your own lives as you reach out and touch those who would appreciate your gesture of kindness and concern... and all that comes with that...

we are aware that many of you do send your monies to those who are doing the work... and we can appreciate all that your gesture does... in addition what we are asking is for you to try and reserve some time during the day to think about where you are... how valuable your life is to you... and where the many others are... who are desperate and discouraged... and reach out to them on a spiritual level... sending them your love and respect for how they endure each and every day...

these wonderful thoughts will be felt by them as they continuously build and flow throughout the lands... the vibration will connect with their vibrations of hope and worry... and will help in bringing them the appreciation for who they are and all that they are doing to survive...

SEPTEMBER 30

These moments in time are just a blink of an eye... for they too shall pass and be remembered only in the way people embrace what it is they want to remember... and how they want to remember it... for the future will be represented by the past... as there is truly nothing different in the future that has not been lived in the past... the future in your lives will depend on what part of the past returns... and of course when you think of what will determine your country's path...

it will be your choices of those who both believe they have the proper answers for the transitioning in the future of your country and all the peoples living in it... both are capable of empowering the country to be better than it has been in the past... according to their beliefs... and there may be truth in both sides of the fence... yet without the proper balance... things will remain lopsided... and unfinished...

it will be very difficult to complete the entire picture each one of your leaders has adopted... for both will have a difficult time... in both convincing the population of their changes to be and for the population to accept them... as there are equal sides of thinking in your world today...

you are truly divided equally... based on what you are receiving now and on what you desire your future to be... depending on the outcome of the winning side... those who are receiving now what they need to benefit themselves may lose all that they strived for... and those who have not received as much will be looking forward to bringing economic rest and development to balance what has been lost for their families and friends...

yes it is an equally diverse group... both seeing their desires in different ways benefitting the country... it will be up to you... the people... who live in your country... on all different levels of life... to decide how they want their country to run... that will affect how you live your lives and the many lives to follow... history does repeat itself... many times over and over... and the results can remain for many a year... before the pendulum swings totally to the other side... after all... it took many years to swing to where you are now... resulting in the chaos and consternation you are living in...

the history of today occurred many years ago... when times were simpler... with less outside influence from the world beyond... unfortunately... at this moment in time... outside influences have upset the delicate balance in the way your country is running... bringing in deepening issues of mistrust... lack of confidence and inaccurate information filling you with inaccurate perceptions connecting you to your vote...

be wise... and find the time to sit quietly... and just feel what your world feels like to you... try not to color your feelings... or question them... as you just sit quietly and allow your higher awareness to open you to the realities of the importance of your vote... each and every vote... that will allow you to think of not only how it will affect you... think of how it will affect your community...

your family... your country and the world... for it is like a house of cards... each part of the world relying not only on themselves... for in order to think of themselves living their lives... they must be able to connect to other sources... for food... materials and protection... as more and more peoples connect with each other in at least a thread of commonality... life becomes more balanced... and less lopsided... as those connections become stronger... life becomes less questionable... more trusting... more accepting of who you are and what you have for yourselves and your families... and so it goes... until like a house of cards... there are certain portions of the world who do not want to connect... by even a thread.. and the weaknesses start to befall the house... the cards can no longer sustain themselves... and fail due to the lack of strength they had in their unity with each other...

as we said... in your world today... the history of the past is not even close to what is happening in your lives today... and due to all these outside factors... as well as deeply untrusting internal maneuvers springing up each and every day... the turmoil is there within you and around you... just as we are... to help you to bring a keener perception... a more comfortable balance and the patience as you live with the knowing... as it is today... and that these times too will continue to evolve into a more balanced and neutral place of living... change is always difficult... yet as we know... life will go on... changes will no longer feel like change and the course of your world will begin to quiet itself and be more accepted...

OCTOBER 6

Is it not a bumpy world sometimes... do all things go smoothly in your world... do you plan your day and find that it is not following your plan... and feel it's bumpy... not easy... more difficult than you expected... and so you view it as a bumpy day... not perfect... not according to what you want...

we are trying to bring you to a place of tapping into your big picture... seeing not that each thing as going off track in your day... and try to see it as being on track... for each part of your day is bringing you to a part of yourself you may seldom use... that of your higher awareness filtering into all things imperfect... sometimes bringing you to your knees... feeling helpless... for you are losing control of your situations... and for what you may say...

what is the purpose of feeling helpless or even feeling your day is not going the way it should... this may sound like a mish mosh of repetitive sentences and thoughts... we are doing this in this way for you to feel the confusion even in this part of the writing... nothing is clear... everything is beginning to sound like gibberish and with no finality... no answers... and yet... there are moments in your life where there is no point... where there just is... that place that comes up when you don't even notice it's beginning to happen and you just bump into it and say... what was that… not realizing that it is just the beginning of a day that is going to be different than you planned…

and then little by little you begin to notice your path is taking you to directions you did not plan on going… neither here nor there… and it may seem random with no value… yet here you are walking along a path that is veering from one way to another… with no mental street signs… just aimlessly walking… feeling you are not achieving anything… again.. we know we are seemingly rambling… and as you can see... words can ramble as well as people moving in a rambling direction…

here it comes… sweet loving and adorable sanity… words that make sense and sentences that have a purpose… we are feeling light hearted today… and want you to share in our lightness… there is no path that goes directly from A to B… in fact most paths never make it past E F or G… and one in a million make it to Z… and those people who make it to Z have lived many lives in their one material life… and carry with them more knowledge than your books … for they are not just writing down the words… they are living each and every one of them… good… bad… and indifferent in your conscious awareness and what they truly lived is touching on their higher awareness each and every day… for their thought process was one of gentle surveillance of all that was around them… all they walked through… and all they survived… as they were absorbing what they saw… and heard and spoke… they were also able to go inward… and touch upon their inner self that is connected to universal consciousness… and reap the rewards of feeling the genuine qualities of all that came to them…

with respect and honor and dignity… they embraced the tiniest to the largest … the least significant and the most important… the boundaries they broke through… and the walls they helped to build to help others protect themselves... and they held themselves up to the consequences they withstood to raise themselves above the natural tendencies to turn away... ignore or deny or just dismiss what it is that made them uncomfortable...

guilt melted away from them... anger melted away from them... reason melted away from them... and feelings were the only thing they held close through their lifetime... for they knew that is where the truth lived... in their hearts and connected to their soul... they followed their path to their winners circle... knowing they had reached the point of bliss... pure... uncolored... untainted... untouched bliss... and knew they would always remember that moment when they reached that point... for it shook them to their roots and that is when they stopped... knowing they were more easily going to return to their A and begin again... only to travel again on a journey filled with the knowing that would take them on their paths of many to live through their material world with grace and love for all...

and would help to deliver that higher love and adulation for all that is within mankind... to all those who enter their path... for no special reason or benefits for themselves... only to bring a small part of what they would feel emanating from them... so that they may share that with others... and eventually bring the material world to a place of nirvana if you will... that place of a higher essence of who you all truly are...

we feel the love that lives within you and chose to write this today to share our love with you through the words... we hope you embrace this writing and that this writing will put a smile on your face for your day... imprinting that feeling that made you smile for the many days to come...

OCTOBER 7

What does it mean when you ask us bring to you whatever you feel you should know… do you know what you should know… do you know what has value for you… or is it to bring to you what you want to know… and were somehow avoiding the information… leaving it to us to prompt you with a thought or a vision or the words…

we understand that there are times when it may feel difficult for you to focus on what is important for you to know and often need some support in getting you started… we understand you may even fight the process or halt the connection before we have completed the information… the method of us coming through to you and you being able to feel us through our messages… visions… astral travels… is difficult in itself… and yet we feel it is important for us to be with you… each and every day to help you to understand that our connection to you can bring you the peace and balance in your life you are all struggling to receive…

we are collectively a universal encyclopedia filled with all knowledge of those who have lived in the material world… and ultimately have converted the knowledge to wisdom as we bring the information to you in a way that will feel comfortable… do not be concerned when we say it is a difficult process... that does not mean that the process will cease or come to you less and less... we are just saying that without a doubt... we are with you always... even when you are not aware of this... to bring to you the feelings of comfort and acceptance of our connection... and will continue to do so until you cross over...

we are in your corner at all times... always letting you know we are with you... in many ways... whether it be an abstract happening in your day that no one can explain... a full blown vision in what you will call a dream... an astral travel (also called a dream) where we take you to a place you may need to see to confirm something you have been thinking about... a beautiful picture of something you have drawn and may not understand where it came from... a song you may have written and as you listened to, began to realize the words did not necessarily come from you... even though they came through you... or these writings that are brought to you through Nadya...

we are your co-partners in life... filled with the information that is available to you at any time... your responsibility is to work with us in adjusting yourself to receiving what you are asking for... without judgment or doubt that it is the real deal... and even in all this... we respect your privacy at those times when you wish to be disconnected... it is all in your hands... as you ask the questions... so shall you receive the answers... and if it feels it is taking too long a time... it is only because you are still not comfortable with the connection... do not ponder on this too long... for it will change... as all things do...

we are asking you... for your own comfort... to be consistent... and the connection will ultimately improve... do not be disappointed or disgruntled... just be... and you will one day know that we are standing right next to you... keep the faith in your own selves... as you start your newest journey into the world of spirit connection and know that we are only here to improve your lives... for your highest good... so that you may bring to yourselves and all those around you a brighter picture... more consistently and without question... doubt or fear... so that ultimately your community and all those communities of the world will be able to live with the peace... harmony and the balance you all so richly deserve... we are happy to meet you all... and are looking forward to working together when you are ready...

OCTOBER 21

Today is Sunday... a day to worship the sun in ancient times... for their sun was their pillar of strength... it grew their crops... it brought them heat... it was their clock and calendar...it allowed their bodies to run themselves with balance... it dictated when to eat their foods... whether it be morning or at night... it indicated when to sleep and when to wake... it brought them feelings of wellbeing... yes... the ancients had their ways of providing what they needed for survival...

have you ever wondered where those thoughts of survival and how to do so came from... was it more of a tried and true test on a daily basis... or possibly a thought that came to their minds suddenly... out of the blue... that helped them to open to something they had never experienced before... that the sun did not just rise and fall... it brought to them many formulas that enriched their lives...

did you ever wonder how it was that people invented things for not only something that was needed... they also invented those things that did not have a need until they realized that once they designed it... the need became clearer... in other words... if you aren't aware that there is a need for something... why and how would you invent such a thing to be used...

and so we go to that path of higher awareness in your growth... those who live in the space you call universal consciousness... are collectively available to you at any time for the answers you may need... or we may see that at a point in your lives... there is an area in your life that may need adjustment... and we step in quietly with a thought... for you to implement as you begin to see what needs to be added or changed or eliminated...

our world runs on vibration... a vibration filled with knowledge that we can convert to you when you ask us in an obvious way or just think about something that you would like to deal with and have not been able to figure out... your thoughts or questions also run on a vibration that streams out into the ether world looking for a source to get an answer and simply put... that stream will connect to a like vibration... bringing to you the answers you may need... in a way that may be less pronounced and more subtle... so it may not be obvious that your thought may not have come from you directly... or many times we are truly abrupt... as there may be an urgent need for you to know something that will prevent you from harm or emotional pain and we see the way to bring it to you more quickly and less subtly... so that you grasp the message... sometimes almost instantly...

truly... we are always here for your highest good...and will never bring to you anything that is not in your best interest... and in a way that is usually comfortable for you to receive... as we certainly do not want to upset you in any way... once you begin to work with us more often... you will begin to see the moment that the switch turns you from off to on and you become more comfortably able to connect with us...

we will bring you more on this subject as time goes by... with much love and adoration for all of you whose desire is to learn how to receive the information for not only your own highest good... alas we are hoping that you will pay your knowledge forward and share it with your communities as well... and as you continue to work with us... your vibration itself will begin to speed up... moving faster... so that it will become easier for us to connect with you... so that you will become more comfortable working with us at any time of your day... week... month or year... for time is not an issue in our world... we work in the past... present and future and hope to be working with you in these times of great anxiety and chaos... bringing to you the peace and balance you all deserve and righteously so...

NOVEMBER 3

It is not without hesitation that we bring to you this writing today... for it may feel a bit more serious than we have written in the recent past... yet it is important to know that living in the material world is but a second in time... it is a life burst of sorts... as you push out into the world and in seconds must take your first breath... at the same time adjusting to the numerous things in an environment you never experienced before... it would feel like a different world than you came from... that you nested in.... and yet you are expected to be a human being who can connect with the people who brought you into this world in a very short period of time...

you are expected to feel comfortable wrapped in a tight cloth against skin that has never been touched before... you are expected to breathe and swallow and see and hear and understand taste all at the same time... you are expected to remember and imprint the first person who held you and expected to feel that this person is important to you as... not knowing what a caretaker is and the importance of it all... you are expected to instantly forget where you originated from... where you grew into what you look like...

yet there is a connection that connects you to your birth and your crossing back to where you came from... that is the tunnel you come through to be able to live in the material world and the tunnel you go through as you enter the parallel world right next to you… it is the biggest rite of package you will ever encounter… for it brings you full circle from your roots and back to your roots... your spiritual roots…

yes… you are all spiritual beings… bringing your light within with you from the spiritual world and carrying it back into the light as you return to the spiritual world… the in between is but a flash in the pan… a stitch in time… a blink of an eye… brought to you for your understanding of what it takes to live as a material being… the happiness and the sadness… the difficulties and the ease of it all… the in between is but a piece of your puzzle in the very big picture of your development… of understanding human frailty and strengths… and to begin your personal journey to develop those characteristics so that you may extend your knowledge to others…

always understand the balance in giving and receiving… whether it be material objects or emotional and mental healing… it will be whatever your gifts allow… and you will learn to feel the satisfaction that comes from helping another to change the direction they are going… seeing a positive outcome… and also feel grateful that you had the opportunity to do so… for it is not only what you give of yourself… it is also what you receive from giving of yourself… without thought as to what you would receive from that…

it is learning to live with a healthy ego… that brings to you humility and acceptance for the things you cannot change… for every encounter you make… you will learn to be aware of the purpose and intention for what you are about to do… and question whether the outcome will change anything and if it does... will it be for the good of all involved... and not just one...

you will begin to observe... to step outside yourself... and watch how you interact with others... is it helping you more than it is helping the others... do you see the reason for why you are helping others... whether it be one or many... are you able to stop yourself from taking that helpful step before it happens... as you see the end result and will know that it is not for you to be involved... yes life in the material world is your biggest classroom... filled with everything needed for your healthy and happy growth and development... to bring you to that higher awareness as you step into the knowing... that place of understanding the balance in all things... large and small...

we understand it will not be easy... for we know that you are delicate... sensitive and sometimes misunderstood and that you struggle to make yourself think only the positive and forego the negative... yet we want you to know that living with both is a healthy balance... as you begin to understand the importance of it all... not one thing is better than another... there is no judgment... other than in your own minds...

as we said... all things are equal... you live in your own personal laboratory filled with every experiment needed to bring harmony and balance to your equation... living in the material world is your portal into the knowing... for experiences are what teach you knowledge that will bring to you the wisdom that will take you to the knowing... and once you have achieved the knowing... you will feel as close to your internal light as you can be ... and will know that what you are feeling at that point is a fraction of how beautiful and wonderfully expansive it will be when you connect to your entire spiritual family who live in the universal consciousness of it all...

NOVEMBER 4

It is truly a far better world out there than you can imagine... for the majority of the people living in the many lands of the world have much in common... they are dreary from living under government rules that prohibit the freedoms you all need to feel motivated about getting up each morning and beginning your day... many of these people are impoverished... and filled with illness that is not being taken care of properly... if at all... many wake each day worried about walking from their humble abodes to a place where food may be bought if they can wait in line for hours to buy it... many are living in fabricated homes... tents or caves or under trees... worried about being kidnapped or killed or raped or tortured by those who are in power at this time... and then there are those who live with dignity... waking each morning to the prospect of either going to their offices or their own place of business to eke out a living... on whatever level it may be... no matter their economy or their own personal fortunes...

those that have not... still feel the same emotions as those that have... those that have not still feel their anguish at not being able to shift from where they need to be to where they want to be... to their fears of waking one morning to find out that one or more of their children were kidnapped through the night... as predators prey on all levels... they worry about trying to sustain a life for themselves as well as for their children... and will give up all they desire to satisfy the desires of their children so that they may see their happy faces...

we understand that you may not realize that the many who have nothing have hope and pray for a better future... and that is what motivates them to continue to learn to be content with where they are... and take even only one step forward each day... keeping that flame of hope and freedom from servitude and anxiety and the injustice of mankind...

that flame within is your spark that lights within you bringing to you the thoughts of a better time... and there are the many guides who live in spirit who are also around you who bring to you those messages that will keep you moving in a positive way... you all have these things... your soul has been with you since you were born... and the guides that are with you each day... may come in and out of your energy field and some may have been with you for a very long time...

these energy fields of higher awareness bring to you comfort and the knowing that there have been trying times before and there will be trying times again... and we are saying this about all aspects of life... wealthy or impoverished... bringing to you the path that you may walk on to successfully achieve the peace you need to find the balance in your lives... and even when you find balance... it may be a momentary thing... for it floats as you do in your daily life of perceptions and expectations...

we understand that living in the material world can be difficult at different times in your lives... we also want you to know that we are with you always and will always be available to you when you are ready to open to that part of you that will bring in the light... guiding you on your path towards a higher... brighter and more accepting and less frustrating day... when it is the right time... just reach out with your thoughts and we will be there... with love and respect for who you are and what you are capable of being...

NOVEMBER 29

It is a dragged out day... yes there are days that can drag... from one minute to the next... from one hour to the next... from one day to the next... and then you begin to see a week has gone by... a month and even a year... and wonder where did that time go... how could it all have happened that quickly... what made it happen that quickly... why did it have to happen at all...

what truly makes time important to you... did you ever wonder why you live by the minutes and hours of each day... we understand it is necessary for scheduling the place that you work in... as it affords you your livelihood... other than that... what would you put next on your list of something that needs to be guided by time... how would you feel if there was no guide of time... other than the seasonal changes in temperature or crops... can you even imagine where you would be in your life without a clock... watch or any other designated time piece that manages you each and every hour of your day...

think about what your schedule would be if you did not have to make money to live your life... what would you do with all the time available to you... it may seem easy... does it not... yet... you might be surprised to know that all that seems easy is not always comfortable... you would first want to learn to feel comfortable when you no longer have to do something that is considered productive... you would need to learn to feel less guilty about not doing something productive... you would want to learn to embrace your life as it has changed enormously... which would include perhaps... a change of location... change of friends and admirers... change of your physical environment...

it would be similar to being of average income and average lifestyle... and suddenly being catapulted into an arena of instant gratification... when many times before you would have had to struggle to achieve what you needed or wanted... you now can reach out and touch whatever you want and it's yours... and then after all is said and done... there is another part of you that could suddenly emerge victorious... that part of you that has been with you since birth... the spirit that lives within... who suddenly becomes a very important part of your conscious life...

for you are just beginning to realize that all the material things in the world are not necessarily going to bring you lasting peace... it will be more or less that all of it may suddenly feel like an interruption in what you knew to be true... and once the dust has settled... you will have a choice... you can either go blindly into that place of self-gratification or you can begin to allow your inner self to emerge... to connect with your conscious self... on a higher level that you have ever felt... enjoying the connection of learning how to separate the important things in your life from the unimportant... and learning to balance what is old with what is new... collectively coming together in your newfound happiness... bringing the peace and balance you no longer will have to struggle for... now that you have learned to love yourself for all that you are... not just the bits and pieces... and want to share that love for yourself as you spread that love to all those around you... near and far...

it is our belief that everyone has deeper points of interest within them... that they either have not recognized or are not ready to open to them... many times it takes either losing everything or receiving everything to realize there is an imbalance... and that you are ready to make peace within yourself so that you may rise up above the emptiness that lived within you... the uncertainty that you would always question and the desire to be happy that was always just beyond your fingertips...

the time is now... to reach out for that happiness... and embrace the feelings of joy that the knowing that has and always will be with you... is within you and around you and just waiting for you to express the desire to embrace it... to accept it... to appreciate and love it... and to bring it into your everyday life... every minute... hour... day... week ... month and years... while you are in the material world and after...

DECEMBER 2

Have you ever thought about the saying all good things must come to an end... would you want those good things to come to an end... would you be satisfied completely with what they have brought to you... and no longer feel as if you needed them any longer... would you even know that those things were good for you... how much attention would you have given to them...

if something is truly good for you... it may seemingly end if you have achieved a finished product or project and reason that it is now over... yet what you call completion is not necessarily so... it may feel that way because of the amount of time you have lived with those good things... yet... time is irrelevant as the energy of those good things will continue to move... and bring you to the next step in the evolution of those good things... what you may call reactions to them or connections that occur from them to other good things...

usually good things attract other good things... whether they be your mental outlook... physical changes or emotional healing... once these things have developed... your higher awareness will begin to bring to you a new outlook on your life... where it is today and where you would like it to go... suddenly you may feel uplifted and less burdened... or perhaps feel less drudgery in what you have been doing... perhaps you may find people to be more interesting than they were before... and even find that you are open to meeting new people with different interests that you would like to learn about... you may feel more physically active... and want to sit less and move more...

there can be a carousel of changes... coming to you in all forms... that have waited for you to open to accepting change... in small ways at first and then larger and larger as you begin to feel more comfortable... and these changes in your life will feel less foreign to you and more intriguing... directing you to being more flexible... less negative... more adventurous and less fearful... more accepting and less challenging... all this with the promise of bringing you to a place of more comfort... more sensitivity to others as well as accepting yourself more easily with less doubt... fear or questions...

you will begin to feel perhaps in the beginning a little offbeat... as how you think and feel may feel a bit foreign to you... and yet these things you are feeling about yourself and others have always been a part of you... waiting to be noticed when you were ready... for all those good things have begun to come into your life as you yourself have chosen to want them and accept them in the place you are in at this moment in time... you have grown and look forward to developing that growth each and every day... with no end in sight... only a change in direction every once in a while... perhaps taking two steps forward and one step back... allowing the old patterns to return more seldomly... until... like a caterpillar... you shed your old skin and feel totally comfortable in being the beautiful butterfly you have become... radiating with the light within you... as you show the world the beautiful you that you are...

we are with you to support your every thought... and are available to help you at any given time... for we are those guides who have been writing with you for all these years... to help you express to the world at large all that you have been... you are today ... and will be in the future... as you walk your path of destiny... so we walk with you... forever in time... with love and devotion... we wish you everything you need to continue on your journey of health and happiness... mentally... physically... and emotionally... we are your biggest fans....

DECEMBER 16

Have you ever felt that a day feels like any other day... and that you can expect what you receive each and every day before that... do you feel that there is no charge to your day... that you are dependent on unexpected things happening to wake you up... snap you out of it... whatever it may be..... for you have never really thought to do those things yourself... to bring excitement... interest... charisma... awareness on a higher level than most days... why is that...

why is it that you feel you may need someone or something to bring you to a point of adulation for where you are on in your day... do you want to think about that for a moment... does this day feel like any other day you have lived... does it feel like yesterday or last week or last month or last year... can you truly remember how those other days felt to you... stop for a moment and think about this... can you actually feel your day...

can you feel the presence of a beautiful butterfly freed from its cocoon... alighting on a beautiful flower for a few seconds... feeding itself in all its glory of that moment... can you feel the breeze gently touching your face as the sun is shining down on you... can you hear the trees swaying in the wind... can you remember how it feels when you hear the birds singing to each other... or their newborns in their nest chattering away as they fight for their food their mother is dropping into their mouths... can you remember the moments of that early morning walk you took when the world was still asleep... and you heard nothing... you were listening to nothing... how did that feel... did it comfort you or make you uneasy... and can you remember those moments... can you go back to how they felt... did they bring you happiness... joy... peace... balance... hope... sensitivity... or did they bring you disparity... forlorn... sadness... uneasiness... aloneness... and a feeling of being disconnected...

we are bringing these things to your attention to bring to you the awareness in all that you do... so that you may feel that anything you do is important and necessary for you to connect with your higher awareness so that you may become part of the knowing... that part of you that can connect with what most people would call insignificant... and yet there is nothing that is insignificant in your day... for life in the physical realm is a daily journey... of touching on all things... reaching out to all things so that you may feel all things... we are not saying this should be done on a 24 hours basis... for you would probably become exhausted rapidly...

we are saying that like a beautiful butterfly... you can touch upon each thing that you notice for even just a second and that would be enough to imprint itself and bring the awareness to the importance of each and every day of your life in the physical world... the days are not to be taken for granted for they become your measuring stick of all that you have learned that you can bring to yourself as well as all those around you... and then disperse that information you have received when you have crossed over... raising the level of your consciousness as you continue to help those in the physical form...

yet even before this happens… your life will become easier as you rise above what was once considered the mundane… and no longer need expectation to bring to you the interest in all that is around you… for all that you need for your own growth… comfort and stability is to feel what is within you… feel all those gifts you came into the physical world with and encourage them to make themselves noticed and available to you … even on a simple level… so that you may practice routinely the exercises of learning to feel… not think… not talk… not touch… just let your eyes find that place of comfort and stay there for a moment… feeling what that moment may bring to you… and carry with you that feeling until the next moment occurs that you choose to accept and feel that moment…

and as those moments continue to grow… it will become easier for you to no longer even see with your eyes… for you will have developed that sense of knowing what things feel like all around you and understand that life is not all about seeing… hearing… touching… or tasting… it is truly about how you connect to all those physical aspects that allow you to sense what you need for your highest good… and leave the rest behind… progressing more easily on your path of destiny… with fewer bumps and less turns… moving straight ahead … with open arms to receive all that comes to you for your highest good…

do not fret if what is considered mistakes are made… for mistakes are your best teachers… and are meant to happen so that you can feel what a mistake for you is… and yet even with that … there are no mistakes… for what could be wrong for you at that moment… can be right in the next… we feel we have said more than enough relating to this subject… we have touched upon it for a short period of time for you to just think about how these words feel to you and if you are ready to begin your journey in a way you have never walked before…

DECEMBER 20

It has been a while since we've written on this day... it is our pleasure to deliver the words to you on this day as well as Sunday... we especially wanted to bring to you today the importance of your need to schedule an appointment with us.. we appreciate your desire to give us enough time to gather the information we direct to you... yet we want you to know that the appointment is more for you than us... we only need a short period of time to gather the words... it is not truly necessary to dedicate a day and time in advance... a few minutes of notice is quite enough for us... as our time runs differently than yours...

we use the word time for you to understand... as we no longer live in time as the physical world does... ours is more of a connection to thought... yours or any other person who wishes to connect to us... it is more of your vibration from your thought that searches for its connection... that brings us to you or any other... for we are a vacuum of information that can move in an instant to satisfy your needs... or any other needs in general... you may want to think of us as a computer of sorts... designed by all who have lived in the material world... to stay connected to the material world by vibration... whether it be mental or physical... speaking that is...

once you think of something that you may want to connect with us about... if you are open and aware of the sensitivities of sending and receiving information... we will bring to you an answer to your thoughts or questions... designed in a way that is for your highest good... for that is our position in your world... to be here to strengthen your connection to your higher awareness so that you may live life on a higher plane of thought... one that will bring you the answers that will satisfy your need to know in a way that will eliminate frustration... anxiety... shallow thinking... so that you can move past whatever the source of all that is causing you discomfort... and bring more light into your world...and the light within you outward...

so all you see will be more easily acceptable from your higher awareness of knowing... bringing you to that place of not living with expectations... and living more with embracing those moments that were once difficult... as you step into that state of blissful understanding of the human element... knowing that this is truly the biggest part of who you are... that is now enriching you with love for yourself as well as all those that may be larger than life or quieter and more timid than a snail...it does not matter what they appear to be... the connection will always be with their inner light... if all of you were introduced to that way of being... it would truly be a beautiful world...

once you begin to connect with all those who are trying to be more connected to their higher self... you will begin to feel even more grateful to those who were difficult... as they have shared their higher energies with you ... charging you in a way... with their inner love... the love from themselves that lives deep within... your knowing that they have identified with that part of themselves is their loving appreciation for you... as you have been enabling a network of glowing love to all those around you and those around them...

we are very happy to send these messages out through you... and the many other light workers in the material world... who are growing larger awareness of emotional healing... as you quiet those who have not yet accepted their higher level of awareness... and bring the world into a more accepting arena of what they once considered differences...

DECEMBER 31

This day is a very special day... for this day ties together all that we have brought to you from this past year to the present... we will end this book of words designed to bring the attention to all things magnificent and all things decadent and all things accepted blindly and all things denied... we are hopeful that these words will have opened the eyes and ears to the harmony one can receive if they live in the moment... even for a second or two... and allow that feeling to imprint itself so that you can extend those moments to reading an entire writing... and as a result once you have completed the writing... will reap the benefits of the higher vibration it brings to you and can discuss its essence as you share the vibration of the words with all those around you...

we are the teachers of the universe... who have projected our thoughts as we embrace the writer... coming in and out of her field during her time of connection to us... there are many who have been with the writer since the beginning of our connection.. and have grown in our numbers with those and the others who enter and pass through as they are needed to present the material...

we are not all from the same generation of peoples... some of us have chosen to live existences unlike others for they live only amongst a small unit of people who practice raising the vibrational bar higher and higher and sending it out to those who need to feel what a higher vibration feels like... and there are the others who prefer to connect with as many people as possible... as they have chosen that field to diligently reach out to as many as can connect with them...

we are joyful that our work is being presented in its entirety... and that none of the details have been changed... it is pure in its delivery and in its essence... we have worked with this writer a very long time to produce this kind of unfiltered vibration... we are joyful that our words are being heard in a broader audience than when we began... and that we will see the words continue in the years to come... for we seek only to bring the harmony of the higher vibration to all those in need and to those who do not feel they are in need... as we have designed our vibration to do so...

we are working in a broad spectrum... with this writer as well as the many others who have seemingly come together in their own way at this time in the world today... to generate love and acceptance for who you are... without judgment or criticism... for it is your essence that we convey in our messages that is the important connection... and not necessarily your physical appearance...

we are sending messages through the abundance of writers today... to help you to not only feel better about yourselves... we are writing to help you to know that in order to do that... change needs to be made... and that you can make those changes that will better your life in small steps... one step at a time... and that once those change are made... you will begin to feel the need to share in your joyful confidence with all those around you... expressing the words of spirit as you connect... and as you become more comfortable with the knowing... that feeling when you go within and trust in what you are feeling... you will begin to bring all those around you more closely... as they will also begin to feel their essence and understand the knowing...

and as you grow in groups and numbers... the numbers will continue to expand as the vibration will feel so good... more and more people will want to understand what they are feeling... and will grow and develop a more productive life... filled with only what is for their highest good... and ultimately war and famine will disappear... as people begin to recognize what is important and what is not... the words are our gift to you... a tool if you will... that will help to guide you on your journey each and every day... bringing you the confirmation you need to want to grow and develop into that person who radiates the light within you...

always remember we are with you always... with love and will be ever watching our truth growing within each and every one of you... as it expands from one community to another... one village to another... and one country to another... we will watch the circle of love growing brighter and stronger as it reaches out to the world... until we meet again... spirit.

ABOUT THE AUTHOR

Nadya Rubin Schubert lives in St. Petersburg, Florida with her husband, Peter, and dogs Shayna and Domino. Originally from Chicago, she has been involved in many creative ventures during her lifetime. Guided by her teacher, Vicki White, she became a conduit between worlds and through release of her books and with her program on the Creating Calm Network, **Notes From Spirit**, she hopes to demystify spirit communications and spark awareness of the connection between the present and eternal lives we live.

www.ingramcontent.com/pod-product-compliance
Lightning Source LLC
Chambersburg PA
CBHW031517040426
42445CB00009B/272